Margaret Wise Brown's Experimental Art

In this study, the engaging art created by children's author Margaret Wise Brown receives the critical attention it deserves as a lasting contribution to American children's literature. Through analysis of her dozens of titles published during the height of western Modernism, this scholarly text shares Brown's importance and impact from the perspective of Brown's work, rather than biographically. Moving beyond such popular titles as *Goodnight Moon* and *The Runaway Bunny* into deeper cuts reveals how Brown's oeuvre bridges multiple disciplines, including writing, visual art, philosophy, and music. Her projects successfully experiment with artistic collaboration and synesthesia as a natural expression for a child readership while both contributing to and reflecting high Modernism amidst the two World Wars. The quality of Brown's writing and the maturity of her themes reveal respect for her child audience and recommend her work to the generations of readers who followed her early death. As this book demonstrates, Margaret Wise Brown remains one of the truly great authors of children's literature.

Julia Pond is Professor of English and Director of the Honors Academy at Shorter University in Rome, GA. She teaches adolescent, children's, and American literatures. She has published articles on topics such as the Harry Potter series, adolescent development in *To Kill A Mockingbird*, and Southern identity in *Children's Literature*, *Children's Literature in Education*, *The Looking Glass*, and *Southern Studies*.

Routledge Focus on Literature

Digital Culture and the Hermeneutic Tradition
Suspicion, Trust, and Dialogue
Inge van de Ven and Lucie Chateau

Dreams in Chinese Fiction
Spiritism, Aestheticism, and Nationalism
Johannes D. Kaminski

Remapping Energopolitics
Blue Humanities, Geophilosophy and Sri Lankan Minor Writings
Abhisek Ghosal

Colonial Philippines in Italian Travel Writing
"Italians" Interpreting Difference
Jillian Loise Melchor

Essays on The Glass Menagerie
Truth in the Pleasant Disguise of Illusion
Tania Chakravertty

Margaret Wise Brown's Experimental Art
The Modernist Picture Book
Julia Pond

For more information about this series, please visit: www.routledge.com/Routledge-Focus-on-Literature/book-series/RFLT

Margaret Wise Brown's Experimental Art

The Modernist Picture Book

Julia Pond

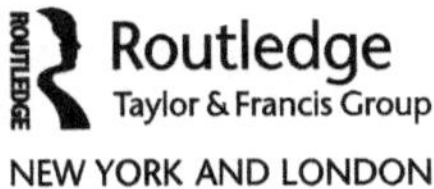
Routledge
Taylor & Francis Group
NEW YORK AND LONDON

First published 2025
by Routledge
605 Third Avenue, New York, NY 10158

and by Routledge
4 Park Square, Milton Park, Abingdon, Oxon, OX14 4RN

Routledge is an imprint of the Taylor & Francis Group, an informa business

ISBN: 9781032727011 (hbk)
ISBN: 9781032727042 (pbk)
ISBN: 9781032727028 (ebk)

DOI: 10.4324/9781032727028

Typeset in Times New Roman
by Newgen Publishing UK

To my grandfather, who I always thought as a child was the smartest person I knew, and who I discovered as I grew up that he actually is. Thank you for inspiring me to learn and study.

Contents

Figures

Acknowledgments

First and foremost, I want to thank God for making my passions and interests into my career. I'm so blessed to get to do what I love every day. He has provided the time and resources to create this study and keeps fulfilling my dreams. I also thank my husband, John David Pond, for always encouraging me forward professionally and celebrating my work when I forget to slow down and acknowledge an accomplishment. As a true partner in life, John David is also responsible for the completion of this work. Thank you as well to my mom and dad, Tom and Kathi Francesconi, for their constant support. Their belief in me makes me reach higher and accept setbacks with determination. I am so grateful to have a strong community even beyond those mentioned, a community that encourages me to live better and seek my purpose with optimism.

Introduction

Readers and scholars often remember Margaret Wise Brown as the author of such nursery bedrocks as *Goodnight Moon* (1942) and *The Runaway Bunny* (1947). Her legacy of dozens of titles is often considered canonical, classic, and foundational American children's literature, standing as a central figure of a time for the American picture book that many scholars now consider its Golden Age. Between 1937, when Brown's first book, *When the Wind Blew*, was published, and December of 1952, when an embolism suddenly ended her life, Brown proved herself a prolific author. Reprints, international publications, new editions, and generic revisions make any specific count of Brown's oeuvre very difficult, but biographers agree that, during her lifetime, Brown completed over ninety picture books, adaptations, translations, magazine stories, articles, and essays, published with nine American publishers, and collaborated with thirty-four illustrators.[1] *Good night Moon* and *The Runaway Bunny* remain her most popular stories, selling the highest number of books and falling among her texts that elicit the most critical attention. Brown's work, however, actually embodies a bifurcated space as posthumous stories continue to be printed, with several slated for upcoming years. Although the greatest volume of her work appeared during her lifetime, her books have continued to appear since 1953, with nineteen texts from eight publishers in the 1950s, five texts from four publishers in the 1960s, one text in the 1970s, two texts from two publishers in the 1980s, and then nothing new released until 2010. In 2010, the British publishing house Parragon Books acquired the rights to Margaret Wise Brown's unpublished manuscripts, and they have since published an additional eighteen of Brown's texts. Sterling and

DOI: 10.4324/9781032727028-1

HarperCollins have also worked with Brown's estate in the past several years, either releasing new material or re-releasing classics with new illustrators. In this way, Brown defines both an historical and a futuristic children's experience, bridging, at this point, almost ninety years of publication and five generations of child readers. Brown is the author of historical, contemporary, and futuristic children's literature, her topics and themes applicable to decades of childhoods. In addition, although Brown herself has been absent for over sixty years, her writing was considered experimental and cutting-edge during her lifetime as it combined childhood study theories of traditional turn-of-the-century pedagogies with ideas from the Bank Street Experimental School. Although the pedagogy practiced by the school and other child development theories have evolved since Brown's tenure at the school, Brown's texts, many of which were heavily influenced by her experience at Bank Street, continue to circulate and to be published due to their popularity with contemporary readers. The continued and then renewed interest in Brown's work raises questions: Why haven't her books become old-fashioned? What about Margaret Wise Brown's writing remains interesting even to contemporary readers?

Margaret Wise Brown contributes empathy, pleasure, substance, and volume to American children's literature, but her central value is her respect for child readers and their art, a respect that continues to draw an audience. While working from a tradition of didacticism through fantasy and practicing realism with Lucy Sprague Mitchell, Margaret Wise Brown moved seamlessly among genres and styles to create art for children that acknowledges their ability to read sophisticated texts and to understand a complicated world without the distraction of overwhelming pedagogical impulses. Her desire to reflect children's experiences in creative, artistic ways demonstrates her high regard for their cognitive and emotional abilities, which produced literature that continues to be read and appreciated long after her death. This esteem led her to mine her contemporary Modernist movement as she experimented with ways to convey subjective experience. She spoke to children through multiple genres and mediums, reflecting the synthesis of art needed to express a child's varied encounters with the world. This goal, and the success of its expression, keep Brown's texts current and beloved.

Rather than expressing ideas in simpler modes for simpler readers, Brown's work expects young readers to rise to the occasion, to enjoy and explore art. This approach removed the impetus for direct moralizing and encouraged audiences to read sophisticatedly, to interpret and to think critically even as nursery-aged children. Charles Baudelaire, a French poet and critic whose ideas greatly impacted the literary atmosphere in which Brown worked, argued that

> genius is nothing more nor less than *childhood recovered* at will—a childhood now equipped for self-expression with manhood's capacities and a power of analysis which enables it to order the mass of raw material which it has involuntarily accumulated.
>
> (8; italics in original)

For Baudelaire, great art might be achieved if the artist were able to rediscover her childhood analytical abilities, the faculty of expressing experience from a place free of connotation, association, or judgment. This goal certainly influenced Brown as, " 'to be a children's writer,' she said, 'one has to love not children but what children love' " (Marcus *Margaret* 251). Brown's impetus to represent the world of her young readers, whose subjective experiences differ greatly from adults', called her to strive for this "genius."[2] In his famous essay, now commonly referred to as a foundational Modernist text, Baudelaire calls for artistic genius to focus on representing modernity, "the ephemeral, the fugitive, the contingent, the half of art whose other half is the eternal and the immutable" (13).[3] This imaginative aesthetic prioritizes the free associations of a childhood he romanticizes, and this skill of Margaret Wise Brown's would firmly, according to Baudelaire, situate her as a modern writer.

Dates and definitions of Modernism are as plentiful as the articles and books written about it. Jed Rasula's more recent work on Modernism lists 1900–1916 as early modernism, the 1930s as late modernism, and 1922, the year T.S. Eliot's *The Waste Land* and James Joyce's *Ulysses* were published, earning "star billing" (1, 2). He lists these dates, however, to show how Modernism actually resists strict dating:

> Assigning 1922 a foundational status privileges a single generation, whereas modernism was indisputably a multigenerational affair. To reduce modernism to a generation collapses it to a biological bulge like the baby boom or consigns it to the symptoms of mass behavior like the Roaring Twenties. Pinning a date on modernism risks reducing art to the artless by-product of fashion

> and historical determinism, a condition that undoubtedly applies to most art in any period.
>
> (Rasula 3)

Other scholars certainly support Rasula's argument that relegating Modernism to certain decades ignores its manifestations over centuries. In fact, Romanian literary critic Matei Călinescu's work on Modernism took him back to the Renaissance where "the opposition of 'modern/ancient' took on particularly dramatic aspects," and, according to his research, it was the Renaissance when "the division of Western history into the three eras—antiquity, Middle Ages, and modernity" first began (19, 20).[4] This resistance to dating moves conversation around the movement toward definition by content or ambition instead. Again, though, Modernism, the Modern, and modernity resist perimeters. Listings of characteristics include "blurring of genre, flagrancy of theme, disobedience to old artistic rules," "an aesthetics of transitoriness and immanence, whose central values are change and novelty," "programmatic agitation (Ibsen, F.T. Marinetti) to a Promethean compulsion to tinker (Picasso, Joyce); from a utopian embrace of new materials (László Moholy-Nagy) to projects of recovering and recycling the past (Pound, Stravinsky)," and, of course, Ezra Pound's emphasis on newness (Albright 37; Călinescu 3; Rasula 16). Not only do these dates and lists range widely in the work they seem to describe, but they often directly contradict each other. Is something modern if it resists the past and tradition, or is it modern if it acknowledges the past and tradition but then changes it, comments on it, re-visions it? Artists and thinkers even self-described as "modern" might answer these questions differently. Finally, then, we are left with ambiguity. As Professor Morag Shiach explains,

> Modernism is constructed through its own contradictions; it is rooted in tradition and classicism but fascinated by the impulse toward the 'new'; it aspires to aesthetic integrity but finds increasingly ingenious ways to capture fragmentation; it presses toward the intensity of the moment but also reaches toward the infinite.
>
> (18)[5]

Margaret Wise Brown's work somehow fits these contradictions; through her wide publication, Brown explored many of these seemingly contradictory concepts in her effort to represent childhood experience.

Certainly, one of the most successful literary tools that Brown employs repeatedly in her writing is synesthesia, a central device of Modernism. Wilhelm Richard Wagner, German composer and conductor, prioritized synesthesia in his music, "indulging in reveries of interchange, the convertibility of one sense into another, seeing sounds and hearing colors, for instance, from which artistic consequences became evident" (Rasula 18). In describing one sense with the adjectives of another, Wagner and many later Modernist artists sought two goals—to reveal connections between artistic mediums explicitly, and to increase the individuality of each medium separately in its original, distinctive characteristics, with the ultimate goal of producing "total artwork" (Rasula 18). For, while bridging mediums often creates harmony, through synesthesia, "each art was radically transformed, becoming in many respects more distinct, more autonomous, as it solicited a congregation of different senses" (Rasula xi).[6] Daniel Albright's *Untwisting the Serpent: Modernism in Music, Literature, and Other Arts* (2000) calls the "fundamental units" of Wagner's *Gesamtkunstwerk*, his hope for a single, unified piece of art, "figures of consonance" in their ability to create accord and harmony between creative endeavors (6). And the appeal of this wholeness recommends itself in its spirit of cooperation and the possibility it offers individual artistic mediums to lend their assistance to each other in a shared effort to move more closely to full expression. Brown's interest in synesthesia appears in many of her texts, most clearly in the *Noisy Book* series and her collaboration with illustrator Leonard Weisgard. In the wake of such artists and thinkers as Baudelaire and Wagner, Brown arrived on the art scene in New York City following her graduation from Hollins College in 1932. There, she stepped into the height of the Modernist movement, finding the children's book a worthy site of artistic experimentation.

Brown's books, both individually and collectively, represent the larger Modernist movement's urge to experiment, bridge artistic mediums, and see past distinctions to observe the interconnectedness of experience. Her body of work blends the arts, calling for aesthetic sophistication in the child reader. In her collaborations and exploration of mediums, Brown reflected Modernism in her poetic writing, her work with visual artists, her philosophical considerations, and her engagement with music. Her work speaks to a dual audience and juxtaposes themes of individuality and community while moving seamlessly between fantasy, realism, tradition, and surrealism. Brown, like Modernism itself, created not "an elite craft refined in secret but as a complex exchange between artists and audiences" (Levenson 3). This book explores the ways in which Brown practiced synesthesia amid the Modernist movement in pursuit of expressing subjective experience through a child's eyes and the core ambivalence between individualism and community in an American identity.[7] She does this with a respect for her younger readers and the goal of exposing them to and including them in the creation of high art.

This exploration begins in the first chapter, which explores Brown's writing, her playfulness, her dependence on repetition, the particular rhythmic quality of her writing, and its poetic thoughtfulness. Over the course of her writing career, Brown developed a unique writing style primarily characterized by her phrasing, the way she combined prose and poetic genres, a strong sensory awareness, and a propensity for lists. These tendencies appear throughout Brown's work and become hallmarks of her texts that renew reading enjoyment afresh for each new generation. These propensities developed in part, however, through the influence of Brown's education, research, and personal reading. Although Brown had many compliments for Virginia Woolf and Beatrix Potter, her most apparent literary mentors remain Geoffrey Chaucer, Lucy Sprague Mitchell, child readers, and Gertrude Stein. Brown's deep interest in Gertrude Stein's writing at the time, for instance, explains much of her own creativeness in this genre and reflects the deeply Modernist tendencies Brown expressed:

> In her children's writing, Brown remained consistently more interested in the musical nature of language and the rhythmic patterning of words rather than well developed plots; this interest links her picture books with the stream-of-consciousness style found in many modernist texts.
>
> (Susina 117)

As modernist as Brown saw herself, however, many of these same stylistic elements can be found even in Chaucer and the Bible. An inclusive consideration of her literary mentors reveals the wellspring of many of her most successful writing traits.

The second chapter moves from recognizing these characteristics in Brown's writing to looking at how she communicates them through the union of words and pictures in the picture book medium. The visual artists, and the illustrations and paintings they created for Brown's books, most clearly represent Brown's love for synesthesia and its move toward harmonic art. As noted by Leonard Marcus, Brown seemed to collect artists, especially those fleeing Europe and World War II, and to curate their art in her own projects. She sometimes chose artists for specific projects and then other times created projects for specific artists, truly attempting blended products. She provided the canvases for such artists as Jean Charlot, Tibor Gergely, Clement Hurd, Alice and Martin Provensen, Esphyr Slobodkina, Leonard Weisgard, and Garth Williams, all eventually famous artists in their own right. Closely considering the body of work produced by individual artists as they visualized Brown's writing reveals how Brown often chose an artist for a particular idea she wanted to convey, so that a collaboration between Brown and an artist can demonstrate the development of a strain of thought over time, as my discussions of Brown's working relationships with her three most frequent collaborators, Clement Hurd, Leonard Weisgard, and Garth Williams, will demonstrate.

The third chapter of this book explores Margaret Wise Brown's philosophic considerations. For the Modernists, "literature, art, dance, music, fashion, industrial design, architecture—they're all there but hovering just out of reach of one another, like academic departments on a college campus" (Rasula 15). The university bridging these departments, so often, is a common philosophy, theory, worldview. And some of the underlying tenets of Brown's urge to represent the child's subjective experience are her own perspectives on subjectivity and experience, perspectives influenced by philosophical considerations. Brown's work offers its readers exposure to object relations, self-individuation, and relationships to time within and between its pages. While child readers may not be familiar with St. Augustine, Mark Currie, Sigmund Freud, Margaret S. Mahler, or Martin Heidegger, the ideas of these great thinkers find representation in Brown's books. Many of their theories deeply concern childhood experience, children's processes of identifying themselves as separate from their parents, their growing and changing perceptions of time and its effect on their bodies, their relationships to the people and objects around them. In order to express the "genius" of childhood recovered, Brown confidently faces these difficult topics, again exposing her "belief that children are, in some important respects, more aesthetically sophisticated than adults" (Baudelaire 8; Stanton "Goodnight" 8). Her texts expect readers' mature interpretation as they respect the children themselves. Educator Rose Oliver claims that "Fairy tales live as long as they are in accord with some deeply rooted perception of reality," and the timelessness of Brown's stories may very well attribute their longevity to the same accord (86).

Finally, the fourth chapter of this book moves into Brown's love for music. Where much of her writing and its rhythm results in prosody, some writing moves even further into melopoetics. With Wagner's fatherhood of synesthesia as integral to Modernism's view of complete art,

> in the domain of the temporal arts, twentieth-century philosophy blurs differences between spoken language and music. The linguistics of Ferdinand de Saussure, the philosophies of Ludwig Wittgenstein and Jacques Derrida, tend to strip language of denotation, to make language a game of arbitrary signifiers; and as words lose connection to the world of hard objects, they become more and more like musical notes.
>
> (Albright 6)

Such texts as *Fish with a Deep Sea Smile* (1938) and *The Wonderful House* (1950) include refrains that "blur [the] difference between spoken language and music." Indeed, these sorts of experiments sometimes led, even more explicitly, to such projects as picture books of songs, such as *Goodnight Songs* (2014) and *Goodnight Songs: A Celebration of the Seasons* (2015). These works included her collaboration with musicians who helped create music to accompany her lyrics.

Margaret Wise Brown's efforts to represent subjective experience repeatedly led her back to the theme of how one is to live in the world, as an individual, but also of the world, as a community member. She skillfully pulled from multiple theories, artistic ventures, and collaborations in order to represent childhood and "what children love" as faithfully as possible. This culling naturally incorporates aspects of Modernism, particularly synesthesia, whose polyphony more accurately captures subjective life. Her relevance's longevity and value in children's literature remains rooted in her own respect for children and their art, and the quintessentially American problems she confronted foreshadow many child readers' continued future identity markers. Brown's importance in the field and its history, as well as its future, stems from the depths of her writing and its reflection of our lives.

Notes

1 Researchers of Brown's biography, such as Amy Gary and Leonard Marcus, may not always arrive at the exact same number, but Marcus, in particular, asserts these numbers as a minimum (Marcus "Margaret" 54).

2 Many scholars, such as Seth Lerer in his book *Children's Literature* and Stephen Mintz in his historical study *Huck's Raft*, explain that childhood has long been recognized culturally and academically as a distinct biological and even psychological stage although the definition of that stage changes through time: "The definition of a proper childhood [...] range[s] from a seventeenth-century conflict between Anglican traditionalist, humanistic, and Puritan conceptions of childhood; to heated eighteenth-century debates over infant depravity and patriarchal authority; and turn-of-the-twentieth-century struggles between the notion of a useful childhood [...] and a sheltered childhood" (Mintz viii). Such historians trace the history of childhood and its literature as a form of cultural studies to decipher important ideologies of different communities and times.

3 In his book *Five Faces of Modernity: Modernism, Avant-Garde, Decadence, Kitsch, Postmodernism* (1987), Matei Călinescu explains that "It is really important to stress that for Baudelaire 'modernity' is not a 'reality' to be copied by the artist but, ultimately, a work of his imagination by which he penetrates beyond the banality of observable appearances into a world of 'correspondences,' where ephemerality and eternity are one. Since Baudelaire, the aesthetics of modernity has been consistently an aesthetics of imagination, opposed to any kind of realism" (54–55). This imaginative drive also accounts for the fantastical elements of Margaret Wise Brown's work as she integrates them with the more realistic tendencies of the Bank Street School pedagogies.

4 Other scholars, such as Marjorie A. Beale, whose work includes the dates 1900–1940 in its title, argue that the "modern era begins in the late Enlightenment, with the beginnings of bourgeois liberalism, the first stirrings of industrial capitalism, and the ascendancy of a scientific worldview" (1). Clearly, dating this movement results in an ever-widening definition.

5 Even more simply put, "modernity remains an elusive concept, one that defies definition and resists precise historical situation" (Beale 1).

6 Modernist scholar Daniel Albright explains this simultaneous bridging and division of the arts "not as a tension between the temporal arts and the spatial, but as a tension between arts that try to retain the propriety, the

apartness, of their private media, and arts that try to lose themselves in some panaesthetic whole" (33). The danger in this second kind of tension, however, "may lead to a kind of overdetermination and overemphasis, which may in turn lead to a kind of ironizing, which may in turn lead to the disaffiliation of the very arts that are trying to cooperate" (28). Attempting synesthesia idealizes the goal of creating some ultimate artwork that may fail in its very inability to represent anything clear or distinct.

7 Such scholars as Barbara Badar, Leonard Marcus, and Joseph Stanton consider Brown's theme of individuality as a representation of growth from childhood. Stanton explains, "The impulse of the child in Brown's books is almost always toward independence, but the independence of the small creatures is always problematic" ("Goodnight" 15). While these readings offer useful interpretation, they may not extend far enough to access completely Brown's attempts to represent American identity concerns.

References

Albright, Daniel. *Untwisting the Serpent: Modernism in Music, Literature, and Other Arts*. University of Chicago Press, 2000.

Baudelaire, Charles. *The Painter of Modern Life and Other Essays*, edited and translated by Jonathan Mayne. Phaidon, 1964.

Beale, Marjorie A. *The Modernist Enterprise: French Elites and the Threat of Modernity, 1900–1940*. Stanford UP, 1999.

Brown, Margaret Wise. *Goodnight Moon*, illustrated by Clement Hurd. Harper, 1947.

———. *Goodnight Songs*, edited by Amy Gary. Sterling, 2014.

———. *Goodnight Songs: A Celebration of the Seasons*, edited by Amy Gary, Sterling, 2015.

———. *The Fish with a Deep Sea Smile*. E.P. Dutton, 1938.

———. *The Runaway Bunny*, illustrated by Clement Hurd. Harper, 1942.

———. *The Wonderful House*. Golden Books, 1950.

———. *When the Wind Blew*. Harper, 1937.

Călinescu, Matei. *Five Faces of Modernity: Modernism, Avant-Garde, Decadence, Kitsch, Postmodernism*. Duke UP, 1987.

Levenson, Michael H. *Modernism*. Yale UP, 2011.

Marcus, Leonard S. *Margaret Wise Brown: Awakened by the Moon*. Beacon, 1992.

———. "Margaret Wise Brown." *Dictionary of Literary Biography: American Writers for Children, 1900–1960*, edited by John Cech, vol. 22. Bruccoli Clark, 1983, pp. 42–70.

Mintz, Stephen. *Huck's Raft: A History of American Childhood*. Harvard UP, 2006.

Oliver, Rose. "Whatever Became of Goldilocks?" *Frontiers: A Journal of Women Studies*, 2, 3, 1977, 85–93.

Rasula, Jed. *History of a Shiver: The Sublime Impudence of Modernism*. Oxford UP, 2016.

Shiach, Morag. "Periodizing Modernism." *The Oxford Handbook of Modernisms*, edited by Peter Brooker, Andrzej Gasioreck, Deborah Longworth & Andrew Thacker. Oxford UP, 2010, pp. 17–30.

Stanton, Joseph. "Goodnight Nobody: Comfort and the Vast Dark in the Poems of Margaret Wise Brown and her Collaborators." *The Important Books: Children's Picture Books as Art and Literature*. Scarecrow, 2005, pp. 7–17.

Susina, Jan. "Children's Reading, Repetition, and Rereading: Gertrude Stein, Margaret Wise Brown, and Goodnight Moon." *Second Thoughts: A Focus on Rereading*, edited by David Galef. Wayne State UP, 1998, pp. 115–25.

1 The Literary Artist

Margaret Wise Brown's prolific output grows even more impressive considering that she only published between 1937 and 1952, which would average over six books a year.[1] She did not intend a career as book author until her plans of engagement to George Armistead and her rambling college studies both ended. She had seen success, however, with an essay published in Hollins's literary magazine, *Cargoes*, which led to her English professor's, Marguerite Hearsey's, encouragement of Brown to consider professionally writing. Some post-graduation adventures and intermittent writing projects culminated in an application to Bank Street's Cooperative School for Student Teachers in New York City in 1935. Here, she met the founder of the Bureau of Educational Experiments and Bank Street's leader, Lucy Sprague Mitchell. Brown took classes that encouraged her creativity and rewarded her for experimentation, at the same time convincing her that she was not interested in a teaching career. Instead, she started attempting to write for children with the guidance of Mitchell and the feedback of the students themselves. In combining literary techniques she adopted from writers she had enjoyed throughout her education with her teachers' and mentors' feedback at Bank Street, Brown developed a style all her own, a style of phrasing, of rhyme, of mixed genres, of rhythm and pattern, of repetition. And this individual, particular style remains Brown's hallmark, continuing to please the ears and imaginations of contemporary children.

In discussing one of Brown's most famous books, *The Runaway Bunny* (1942), Leonard Marcus writes, "Brown's writing [in this book] is as self-sufficient as any she published—its poise and nobility of phrasing are rare in the literature for the young" ("Margaret"

DOI: 10.4324/9781032727028-2

57). Brown's phrasing, the choice and order of words in her stories, uniquely represents her authorship. In *The Runaway Bunny*, for instance, the phrasing Brown employs creates a game played between the mother and child rabbit characters. For each scenario that the child bunny imagines, his mother responds with a solution that reunites them. If the "little bunny" considers becoming "a fish in a trout stream," his mother replies that she would "become a fisherman" and fish for him. When the child bunny thinks of "join[ing] the circus and fly[ing] away on a flying trapeze," the mother bunny "will be a tight-rope walker and [...] walk across the air" to him. The story constitutes a game of wits, one in which the child protagonist attempts to find situations to elude his parent, but every hypothetical concludes with his mother's promise to find a way to be with him. The phrasing of this story lends it playfulness. The if/then calls and responses provide the book with narrative plot points that child readers can anticipate as well as encourage these potential readers to imagine their own possibilities of escape. This game, however, has a depth to it as Brown's story opens by telling readers that "there was a little bunny who wanted to run away." The book does not explain why the bunny wanted to run away, but it suggests, through the presence of the mother, a rift in the mother/child relationship that causes the little bunny to threaten his mother with his absence. The game's effect, however, assures the little bunny that, no matter what he does, where he goes, or what he tries, his mother's unconditional love will drive her toward him and in pursuit of him, and the game provides healing in their relationship through its engagement of both parties' imaginations and attentions. Readers don't need to know what event or conversation caused this exchange; the exchange itself resolves the problem and reinforces the mother bunny's point of view—she will always chase after relationship with her son.

The majority of the book constitutes this imaginative word game between the little bunny and his mother, but the last two pages resolve any potential tension created by the beginning with a swift turn of phrase. The game relies on more formal diction, such as the mother bunny's explanation that she will "run after" the little bunny, "For you are my little bunny." Rather than stating that she will pursue her child "because" or "since" he is her child, Brown includes the more antiquated "for," which nicely establishes a structure, a formality, a tone in which the following game is played. Both players adhere to the rules, follow the wordplay, until the tone turns at the end with the little bunny finishing, "'Shucks,' said the bunny, 'I might just as well stay where I am and be your little bunny.'" The shift in the phrasing's tone from formal to colloquial signals to readers that the mother has won the game, the relationship has been restored, and the child has rediscovered his sense of belonging and importance. The mother bunny then replies by offering food: "Have a carrot." This gesture of maternal care demonstrates that all has been forgiven and forgotten, and she continues to provide for him. The ending contrasts stories such as Beatrix Potter's *Peter Rabbit* in which the maternal figure withholds food from the young, male protagonist as punishment for disobedience. Instead, *The Runaway Bunny*'s phrasing, even in its brevity, builds a relational world much larger than the small book it inhabits.

A personal favorite of mine, Margaret Wise Brown's *The Wonderful House* (1950) produces a similar effect in its phrasing. In this story, instead of a game of wordplay between two characters, Brown creates a conversation of questions and answers between the text and its reader. Each page posits the question of who lives in the home pictured in J.P. Miller's illustrations. The subsequent page answers the question, showing the person or animal in the home and either corroborating or correcting the imagined child reader's answer. Like in *The Runaway Bunny*, the questions create anticipation as the book continues and the reader learns how to play the game. One of the most fun characteristics of the story, however, is Brown's turn of phrase. At the transition from the first half of the story, which constitutes the call and response half, to the second half, in which the questions concern one particular house that is flying closer and closer through the air, Brown's questions and answers cleverly appear enfolded in the narrative itself. For example, following the answer that it is a "funny little rabbit" who lives in the hill pictured, the narrator asks, "Who lives here? And who lives there? But what is that flying through the air!" The narrator's questions (while the illustrations picture beehives) are interrupted by the appearance in the sky above a truly original home, a house with wings, held aloft by balloons. Now, the readers have two questions to answer: Who lives in the beehives, and what is flying through the air? As the story moves into greater interest in the flying house, the narrator does not fail to answer the question of the beehives as well. The next page reads, "Bees, stop your buzzing! Who comes there?" Brown's phrasing moves the story seamlessly from a general game of guessing in what kinds of homes people and animals live into a specific guessing game of who might live in this one unique home. In addition, the direct address to the bees includes them in the new game by blaming their "buzzing" for distracting the narrator from playing the new version of this guessing game.

Similarly, a couple of pages later, an owl appears as the character to whom the rest of the questions are addressed, and Brown's choice of an owl implies its appropriateness as the animal that is always asking, "whooo?" The narrator exclaims, "What in the world! It flies through the air. Old owl, tell us, who lives there?" The "who" in this question does not need to be bolded or underlined to encourage reading this word aloud as an owl hooting. From this point on, the questions in the text change from "who lives here?" to "Is it?" The rest of the book posits possible inhabitants of this wonderful, flying house, but every question is shadowed by the owl's "whooo?" Once again, the clever phrasing of the questions, answers, and transitions increase the pleasure of reading aloud Brown's book as well as instruct, anticipate, and manipulate the narrative.

Another aspect of Margaret Wise Brown's writing that contributes to her style is her repeated creation of story as poetry.[2] Indeed, children's literature scholar Jan Susina reads *Goodnight Moon* as "a children's illustrated poem" (118), and art historian Joseph Stanton points out that, although

> [Brown] never achieved the success she had hoped for as a writer of poetry or fiction for the adult market, [...] she made the best of her own unique form of literary art—a form of prose poem for children's picture books that could achieve a kind of eloquence for which simplicity of statement was a precondition.
>
> (Stanton "Goodnight" 15)

Most of Brown's writing is, in some way, poetic in nature, but many of her narratives include distinct moments in which the narrative breaks its prose. These moments turn the writing from a more general prose poem to concentrated poetry.[3] For example, in *The Color Kittens* (1949), the narrative of the kittens trying to make green paint is interrupted by short poems, at first about each color they create: "Brush mixed red paint and white paint together—and what did that make? It didn't make green. But it made pink. Pink as pigs / Pink as toes / Pink as a rose / Or a baby's nose." One of the ways in which the text signals the move from prose poem to poetry is by dropping its punctuation.

Although most of the narrative includes rhythm and often rhymes, it is also punctuated. The brief moments of poetry, however, release that punctuation, and the lines are usually scattered throughout the illustrations rather than appearing in formal paragraphs: "Then they mixed red and blue together—and what did that make? It didn't make green. It made a deep dark purple. Purple as violets / Purple as prunes / Purple as shadows / On late afternoons." Similarly, in *Home for a Bunny* (1956), Brown uses the prose poem again when she writes, " 'Spring, Spring, Spring!' sang the robin. It was Spring / The leaves burst out. / The flowers burst out. / And robins burst out of their eggs. / It was Spring." These movements into and out of poetry remain a distinct marker of Brown's enjoyable writing style.

One of the markers of prose poetry, writer Paul Munden argues, is its treatment of time. He notices that "prose poetry's instinct, and effect, is often to shrug off any sense of narrative structure or thrust, and offer instead an ingenious lens through which far-fetched moments can be viewed as part of a single, kaleidoscopic scene" (2). In these sorts of texts, time works differently. Instead of a continual march forward, there is often a collapse of time that happens, a break in time, so that the poetry creates a pause in which to consider a subject without progressing the story. Margaret Wise Brown's use of poetry within her prose poem makes this shift in time evident. In *The Wonderful House*, for instance, the word game between narrator and reader resolves in poetry. The poem covers two pages, in most printings, or at least two stanzas, but it does not progress the story. Following the narrator's answer to the reader's guesses, "No! All guesses are wrong," the poem begins,

> It is a wonderful house
> With wings to fly with
> And wheels to roll on
> And pontoons to float on
> And balloons to hang on
> And flowers in the windows
>
> And a boy and a girl live in this house
> With a dog and a rabbit and a cat and a mouse
> And animals everywhere.
> And they all go flying through the air,
> To where they want to go.

Where the prose poem of the preceding story consisted of the reader getting nearer to the answer of who lived in this house, as well as the time passing that brought the flying house closer and closer to view, the poem that ends the story stops that flow.

Now, the house remains hovering before the reader while a boy is frozen in mid-wave out one of the house's windows, and the narrator takes the time to describe the house in detail. Just as the narrator of *The Color Kittens* pauses in telling the story of how the kittens make green paint to provide poetic interludes, so too does *The Wonderful House* employ poetry as "a kaleidoscopic scene" (Munden 2). This poetry is also more formal in appearance, following a regular meter (with most lines ending in dactyls), using rhyme and anaphora ("And"), alliteration ("wings," "with," "wheels," "where," "want"), assonance ("pontoons," "balloons," "girl live in this"), and repetition ("on," "a," "and," "go"). Brown's prose poetry already pleases the ear and makes reading her books aloud enjoyable; mixing the genres of prose, prose poem, and poetry—not to mention the illustrations—only further establishes her as an artist in her own right.

The Modernist, multi-generic texts that Brown wrote include such a wide array of writing conventions and methods so as to contribute greatly to the writing style recognizable as her own. Folklorist JoAnn Conrad appreciates this variety in Brown's writing: "Her unique writing style incorporated elements of modernist stream-of-consciousness, minimalist texts, lack of plot, heavy repetition, and word play" (140). Brown wrote in prose; she wrote prose poems; she wrote poetry; she wrote songs; sometimes, she let the illustrations do the communicating. Regardless of the genre in which she constructed her stories, though, one of the most commanding characteristics of her writing style is its rhythm. In his 1928 *The Language and Thought of the Child*, Jean Piaget points to rhythm as foundationally important to enjoyable narrative and its role in art. Lucy Sprague Mitchell recognized this very element as essential to all literature, regardless of its intended audience:

> Even [Jean] Piaget [...] suggests that children will soon outgrow the childish pleasures in rhythm and sound qualities and speak sensibly like grownups. And so they do! To Piaget, this dropping of art elements from language is progress, the overcoming of an immaturity. To me it is a tragedy, for to me a child's pleasure in

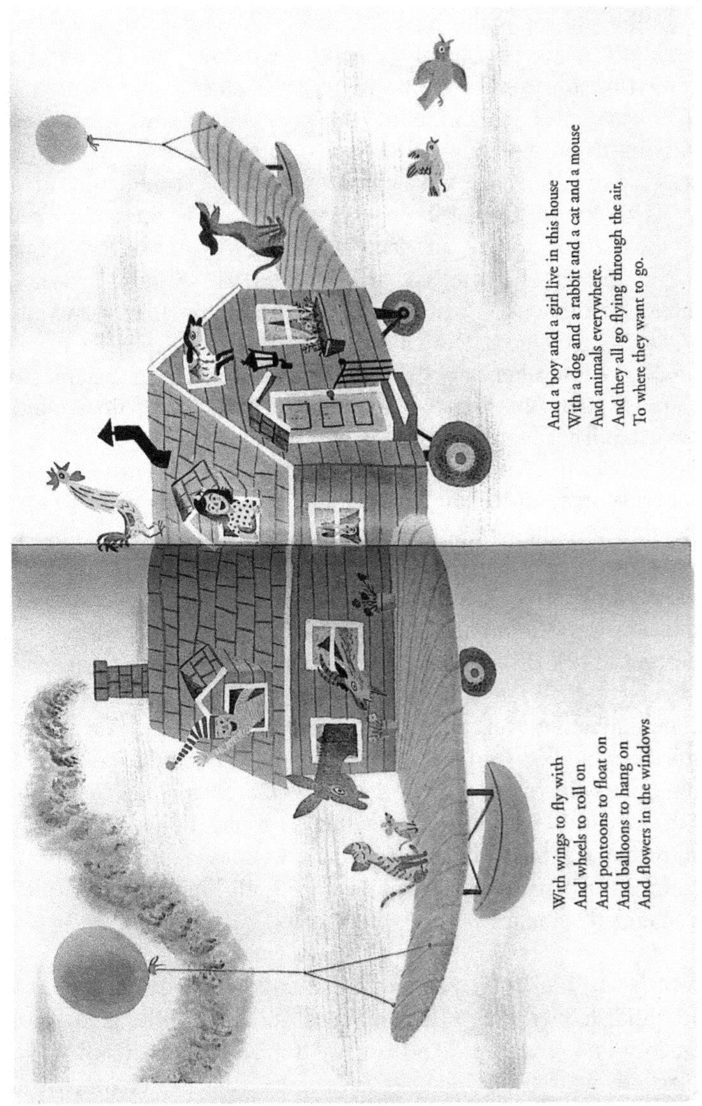

Figure 1.1 Brown, Margaret Wise. *The Wonderful House*. HarperCollins, 1950. pp. 36–37.

> rhythm, sound quality and pattern is the seed from which literature grows.
>
> (Mitchell *Two Lives* 281)

If Mitchell were correct, then a love of literature must grow in many a child's heart who spends time with Margaret Wise Brown's stories. Rhythm drives every episode of Brown's *The Friendly Book* (1954). In "I Like Cars," the cadence begins strong and fast: "Red cars / Green cars / Sport limousine cars / I like cars." But then it slows to include more description: "A car in a garage / A car with a load / A car with a flat tire / A car on the road," which then makes the last line particularly satisfying with its return to the original assertive hit: "I like cars." "I Like Stars" is similar, with the rhythm beginning quickly and confidently: "Yellow stars / Green stars / Red stars / Blue stars," then moving to a slower tempo and greater description, "A star that is shooting across the dark sky / A star that is shining right straight in your eye" and finishing with repetition of the title and a quickly-paced line, "I like stars." These stories are enjoyable in their ability to offer variations on each theme, Bugs, Cars, Seeds, Stars, Trains, Dogs, and People, but also in the meter and rhyme of their diction.

Similarly, *The Wonderful House* creates pleasure in the rhythms it first establishes and then breaks. By creating a particular rhythm, such as in the lines "And who lives here? A nutty little squirrel. He lives here. And who lives here," Brown allows the reader to fall into a vocalization pattern similar to sung lines. When she then continues the rhythm but breaks the word pattern, "And who lives here? Bow wow wow. A dog lives here. Bow wow wow. Bow wow. Meow," the result is playful and energetic. That shift wakes readers from the lulling effect of the rhythm to surprise them pleasantly with something new. In fact, the presence of the final "Meow" provides information that otherwise does not appear in the language of the story. The page illustrates a dog chasing a cat away from his doghouse, quite gleefully, and that action in the plot is present in the story's language only in a single word, "Meow." A page later, the narrative continues as expected, but the rhythm changes: "But who lives here? Deep in the dark mysterious river." Readers have returned to the question and answer form of the book, but this time it is the rhythm changing that provides the unexpected. Returning to the previously established rhythm then re-establishes the pleasure: "I live here. My dear!" By controlling the rhythm, by instituting patterns of word choice and syllabic progression, and then interrupting those anticipated prescriptions, Brown's style remains pleasurable and lively.

Finally, Brown's predilection for repetition and listing contributes to her recognizable writing style. As mentioned above, in Brown's phrasing, rhythm, and pattern of writing, repetition often appears. Sometimes it is repetition that creates the rhythm and that permits a surprising turn of phrase that deviates from an established verse. Other times, the repetition creates comparison. Brown's common, thematic big/little comparisons provide the thrust for several stories, requiring the repetition of words to show the difference between size. In *The Little Fisherman* (1945), pages repeat each other exactly, even in illustration, with the exception of a change in adjective from "big" to "little": "The big fishermen had big sailors on his boat—big sailors with big ropes and big buckets with big scrub brushes and big fishnets and big hammocks that they slept in at night." The following page reads, "But the little fisherman had little sailors on his boat—little sailors with little ropes and little buckets with little scrub brushes and little fishnets and little hammocks that they slept in at night." The repetition of these objects and actions characterizes Brown's "here and now" writing by focusing on the sometimes mundane details of personal life. Similarly, in *A Child's Good Night Book* (1943), each page describes the nighttime routine of a different animal, ending with the same line each time: "The bunnies close their bright red eyes. Sleepy bunnies [...] The squirrels are hidden in the trees. Sleepy squirrels." In this book, the repetition contributes to the lullaby, a verbal rocking motion that creates its own pre-bedtime ritual of soothing and calming. The repetition found in *The Wonderful House* is less a reoccurrence of particular words and more often the repetition of questions and answers. Even though the questions may change from "Who lives here?" to "Is it a circus clown?" or "Is it a curious monkey?" the reader knows to expect a question, followed by time to respond and then receive the answer on the next page. In this case, the particular words are not always repeated, but the book's structure is repetitious, exemplifying a variation of Brown's writing characteristic.

Margaret Wise Brown books also include many lists. The lists might serve different purposes, depending on each book's theme and plot, but they often provide variation on a single topic, examples of types. *The Friendly Book* utilizes lists on every page so that the writing includes the rhythm of the list itself as well as the repetition of lists on different pages, each list often appearing as mini poems among the whole of the book. The page/poem "I Like Stars" reads,

> Yellow stars / Green stars / Red stars / Blue stars / I like stars / Far stars / Quiet stars / Bright stars / Light stars / I like stars / A star that is shooting across the dark sky / A star that is shining right straight in your eye / I like stars.

Likewise, "I Like Fish" repeats the listing of types of fish in poetic form:

> Silver fish / Gold fish / Black fish / Old fish / Young fish / Fishy fish / Any kind of fish / A fish in a pond / A fish in a stream / A fish in the ocean / A fish in a dream / I like fish.

The way that Brown layers her techniques here nicely displays her expressive style.

It could be argued that most of *The Wonderful House* is also a list, a list of questions and answers on the same topic, but there also appears a concentrated list of possible inhabitants of the Wonderful House toward the end of the picture book:

> Is it a walrus's house? Or a lobster's house? Or a frog's house? Or a witch's house? Or a piggywig's house? Is it a giraffe's house? Or a fish's house? Or a hat's house? Or a dog biscuit's house? No! All guesses are wrong.

On these two pages, the narrator stops providing the space to answer the questions and instead, fires them more rapidly to increase the speed of the narrative toward the final answer, "It is a wonderful house." These lists appear throughout Brown's lifeworks, each made appropriate for her topics, themes, and intended readership.

Margaret Wise Brown's writing style combines common techniques to create a strongly individual practice, recognizable as hers among other picture book authors. For a writer who, even through college, did not intend to write, and once she considered the discipline, did not intend to write for children, and expressed herself quite originally, Brown's style developed through the exposure to and mentoring of several people, as well as her cultural and historical context. While these influences include personalities from Chekhov to Emily

Dickinson and the Bible, the strongest echoes in Brown's writing life remain Geoffrey Chaucer, the Bank Street School and, particularly, Lucy Sprague Mitchell, Brown's child audience, and modernists such as Gertrude Stein. These molding pressures also encouraged Brown's specific interests in the child's mind and American identity.

Geoffrey Chaucer

Geoffrey Chaucer (1340?–1400) lived and worked in England under King Edward III and, later, King Richard II as a diplomat and civil servant, although he remains best known today, of course, for his writing. While his earlier works, such as *The Book of the Duchess* and *Troilus and Criseyde*, still appear in critical studies, it is *The Canterbury Tales*, constructed through the late 1380s and the early 1390s, that remains his masterpiece (Lumiansky xxviii, xxii). While he only completed a fifth of what he had planned for the *Tales*, Chaucer's narrative of pilgrims on a trip to the shrine of St. Thomas Becket at Canterbury and the stories they tell each other along the way, even this unfinished work guaranteed Chaucer's enduring place in the English literary canon. In fact, in his "General Introduction" to R.M. Lumiansky's modern English prose translation of the *Tales*, David Williams claims that Chaucer "is the first native English literary authority, and the extent of his authority is unequaled in English literature" (xvi). This authority has retained its strength through Chaucer's appearance in university English classrooms, which is where Margaret Wise Brown spent time studying his writing while at Hollins. This Chaucer class, taught by Marguerite Hearsey, not only instilled in Brown a deep appreciation for Chaucer's use of language, but it also resulted in Brown's first published essay in the university's literary magazine, as previously mentioned. Once an accomplished author herself, Brown continued to refer to Chaucer as her "old master," just as the poet was "repeatedly referred to in the fifteenth and sixteenth centuries as 'Master' by aspiring and established writers alike" ("Creative" 77, Williams xvi). While students of Chaucer certainly learn much about art, history, and life through his texts, Brown's education by Chaucer appears directly in her writing in such literary elements as the musicality of her verse, her use of colloquial speech, and her identification with her own characters.

During the time that Chaucer lived, the English language saw great developments and shifts, particularly in attempts to collapse the linguistic differences between classes and professions as well as to bridge translation errors between the many languages circulating in England. Susan E. Phillips argues that Chaucer used *The Canterbury Tales* to offer solutions to these multilingual frictions (51). Chaucer himself was multilingual and is widely believed to have looked to such French poets as Guillaume de Machaut and Jean Froissart as models for his writing, poets who wrote "lyrics and narratives about courtly love" as well as historical chronicles (David 211). For the reason of recognizing and appreciating the diverse languages and dialects from which Chaucer pulled, many scholars still argue for the need to read Chaucer's work in its original Middle English, rather than in more possibly accessible, modern translations: "Chaucer's poetry, like that of his contemporaries, needs to be read with some understanding of the nature of late fourteenth-century pronunciation if the full musicality of his versification is to be appreciated" (Pearsall 2).

Like Chaucer, Margaret Wise Brown's writing demonstrates concentrated musicality, prose poetry that sometimes bursts into explicit song. Jan Susina considers *Goodnight Moon* a strong example of Brown's lyricism, calling it "a simple poem celebrating the musical nature of verse" and "a lyrical book of leave-taking" (119). Barbara Badar explains that "it was more and more important to Brown, this writing of songs, of poems to be sung" (260). In fact, the idea for and pattern of *The Runaway Bunny* originated for Brown in a Provençal troubadour ballad (Marcus *Margaret* 149). The difference between poetry and music is narrow, sometimes invisible, as most definitions look similar but include the auditory nature of song as its defining characteristic, but there remain two ways in which Chaucer's writing is described as musical that also apply to Brown's writing: first, *The Canterbury Tales* includes many allusions to, intertextuality with, and other references to descriptions of instruments, singing, and varied forms of music. Elaboration on this point has already filled other scholars' book-length projects, but one of the first examples easily referenced is the Host's description of the Squire: "Singing he was, or floiting, al the day: / He was as fresh as is the month of May [...] He coude songes make, and wel endite, / Juste and eek daunce, and wel portraye and write" (Chaucer, "General Prologue," lines 91–92, 95–96).[4] In addition to the Squire's singing and song-writing, *The Canterbury Tales* includes numerous other descriptions of singing characters, instruments, and song. Likewise, many of Margaret Wise Brown's stories and poems describe similar activities. Most notably,

Brown's *The Little Brass Band* (1955) follows musicians through their day as they gather, play for a village, and disperse back to their homes again at night. Clement Hurd's illustrations clearly depict the medieval costumes, instruments, and architecture of a possible fourteenth- or fifteenth-century setting.

Other Brown books include references to music as well, however, such as the birds, frogs, and crickets that sing in *Home for a Bunny*, the organ grinder and the dancing monkey in "The Monkey Man" from *Give Yourself to the Rain*, and all the *Noisy Book* references to the world's music. Of course, Brown wrote books of songs as well, which will be discussed in the final chapter.

Second, Chaucer's verse expresses musicality in the rhymes and rhythms of the words themselves. Pearsall credits Chaucer with

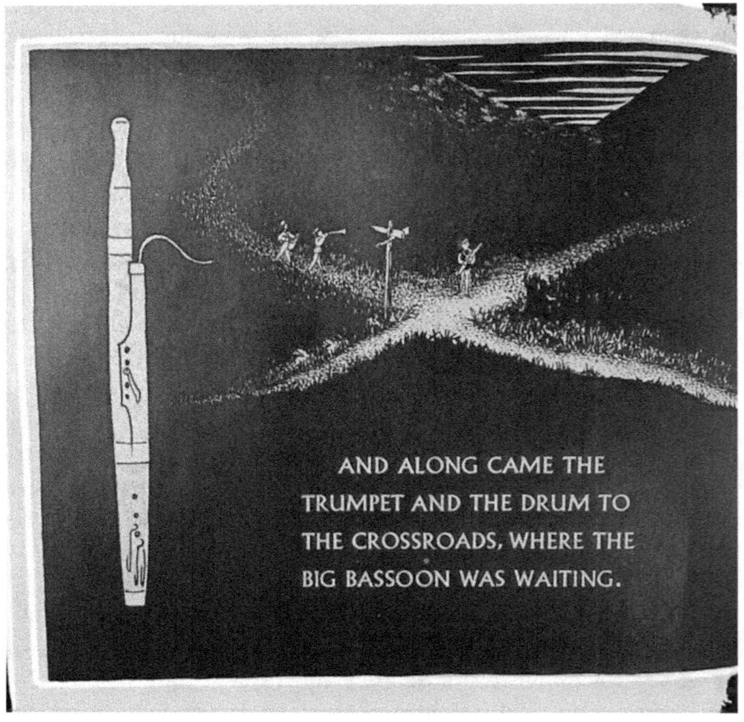

Figure 1.2 Brown, Margaret Wise. *The Little Brass Band.* HarperCollins, 1955. pp. 10–11.

introducing iambic pentameter into English verse, providing much of the singsong rhythm of his lines (2). The argument for reading Chaucer in Middle English, in addition, relies on his rhyme, with "long vowels [...] given their continental rather than their modern English or American values [...] The pronunciation of inflexional final *-e* is vital to the understanding of the music of Chaucer's ten-syllable line" (Pearsall 2). Chaucer does not just reference music; he writes musical poetry. This characteristic may remain a fragment of Chaucer's influence on Brown's writing, as her picture books and poems also display these personalities in rhythm and rhyme. For example, in her poem aptly titled "Song of Little Things" from *Under the Sun and the Moon and Other Poems* (1993), Brown plays with the traditional iambic pentameter by writing iambic tetrameter, three lines of which end in spondees:

> Oh sing a song of little things
> Of bugs and flies and flickering wings
> Of flakes of snow and drops of rain
> And yellow flowers in the lane
>
> Of little pairs of squeaky shoes
> And mice that laugh until they snooze
> Of stars and pins and crumbs of cake
> And bugs that laugh themselves awake.

The poem's rhythmic rocking motion, combined with the rhyming couplets, provides a song-like quality, which Brown clearly intended, as expressed in the poem's title.

In addition to their shared musicality, Geoffrey Chaucer and Margaret Wise Brown share a preference for colloquial speech. One of Chaucer's differentiating authorial techniques, Lumiansky argues, is his diction: "his English is not the language of the universities or the court, except when he wants it to be; usually it is the highly colloquial, everyday language of the streets" (xxxviii). The Host warns readers to expect this divergence in his "General Prologue":

> I beg you in your kindness not to consider me vulgar because I speak plainly in this account and give you the statements and the actions of these pilgrims, or if I repeat their exact words. For you know just as well as I that whosoever repeats a tale must include every word as nearly as he possibly can, if it is in the story, no

> matter how crude and low; otherwise, he tells an untrue tale, or makes up things, or finds new words. He cannot spare even his brother's feelings; he must say one word just as well as any other.
> (*The Canterbury Tales* 16)[5]

The Host's claim points to the necessity of using dialect and diction that most accurately represents the character type speaking in an attempt at truth and authenticity. This approach provides Chaucer's writing a "naturalness and freedom from contrivance" that much other writing of his time did not display (Williams xvii). Similarly, Margaret Wise Brown strove to speak simply and honestly in mimicry of a child's use of language. She wrote, "The key to [writing for children] is simplicity" ("Creative" 77). In Chaucer, we can see this valorization of brevity and simplicity in "The Knight's Tale," which mentions the importance of conciseness at least seven times in such asides as, "My intention is to be brief," "To make the story short," and "as briefly as I can, I hasten to give you the description" (*The Canterbury Tales* 22, 30, 42). Even though his tale is one of the longest, the Knight strives for brevity, a characteristic that also appears in Brown's writing. In *Two Little Gardeners* (1951), for instance, Brown writes lines such as, "Then the sun shone hotter and hotter. No rain." In fact, the first line of the book reads, "Spring!" and then moves on. Brown's use of incomplete or simple sentences reveals her appreciation for colloquial, youthful language over grammatically correct verbosity. The quotation at the opening of her contribution to the 1951 *Book of Knowledge* states, "The written word should be / Clean as bone, / Clear as light, firm as stone. / Two words are not as good as one" (Anon qtd. in "Creative" 77). And where Chaucer's use of simple language is often attributed to his "celebrat[ion of] enterprising poseurs instead of diligent scholars or eloquent courtiers" (Phillips 40), Brown's use of the same kind of language demonstrates an attempt to write the way children speak for the child reader:

> I have always been tremendously interested in and amused by the sheer elements of language, but unless a writer is very lucky this playfulness turns into preciosity and writing for other writers. But when the sheer rhythms and thunders and patterns of language are given back to children then they come into their rightful element.
> (Brown "Creative" 81)

As Brown's "master" in using the English language for writing, Chaucer appears to have influenced her wordage.

A third area in which Chaucer's instruction of Brown appears is their deep awareness and understanding of their own characters and audiences. Brown explains that she often pulled from her memories of being a child as well as the child-self still inside of her in order to write stories that appeal to children: "We all have a child still alive in ourselves who can recognize and meet those qualities of pure childlikeness in another child" ("Creative" 78). Brown understood her audience. Her books remain true even now because she worked to write from her own childlikeness to other children, rather than as an adult with all the power discrepancies and authoritarian clout often present in that role. In his Introduction, David Williams explains that, likewise, Chaucer's understanding of the human continues his influence:

> *The Canterbury Tales* has had an enormous influence on successive writers and audiences because it transmits one of the most brilliant illuminations of human experience—social, intellectual, and spiritual—that we possess" (xv). Chaucer often writes about some of the worst traits of man but does not demean those characters or shame them, as he "possessed tolerant understanding rather than a holier-than-thou attitude.
>
> (Lumiansky xxvi)

In fact, Brown noticed this characteristic of Chaucer's writing and celebrated it:

> 'We […] breathe a sigh of relief' she wrote of Chaucer's robust depictions of human folly, 'to find ourselves exposed in a light that makes us appear much less sinister than did the shadow of our own imagination. Our burden of bad conscience becomes merely a humorous deformity that we share with our fellow-men.'
>
> (Qtd. in Marcus *Margaret* 31; ellipses in original)

Recognizing ourselves in the books we read, feeling known and accepted, facing ourselves but then finding community in those shared traits, these attitudes are purposefully cultivated in Geoffrey Chaucer's and Margaret Wise Brown's writing. Although living very different lives, centuries apart, these two authors share some foundational approaches to their audiences that link their writing practices.

They both combine realism and fairy tales; they both ask their readers questions; they both employ lists and direct addresses. Chaucer left both word-level and stylistic-level influences on Margaret Wise Brown's picture books.

Certainly, Chaucer's influence remains broad, as many writers have been subject to his impression, and Brown's use of specific literary tools may not directly connect the two authors; however, Brown's education in Chaucer, her expressed appreciation for him, and the authorial art she later produced all combine to establish him as one of her literary models. She seemed to think of him regularly through her adult life, once remarking that her 1937 trip to England turned out to be "part of a pilgrimage, half prioress half wife of Bath" (qtd. in Marcus, *Margaret*, 83). Even the Knight's prophetic axiom, that "it is best, from the point of view of fame, to die when one's name is best known," tragically applies to Brown's early death (*The Canterbury Tales* 62). Chaucer, in addition to Marguerite Hearsey, turned out to be one of Brown's writing teachers after all.

Lucy Sprague Mitchell and the Bank Street School

Margaret Wise Brown's most literal writing teacher, however, remains Lucy Sprague Mitchell at the Bank Street School, more formally known as The Cooperative School for Student Teachers under the Bureau of Educational Experiments, which Mitchell ran from 1930 to 1955.[6] This school is where Brown found herself three years after her college graduation at the encouragement of a Greenwich Village friend, Inez Camprubi, who was enrolled as a student at Bank Street. The goal of the school, at that point, was to combine art and science, to use scientific method to discover the most successful ways of creating art. In order to create children's literature specifically, or to teach children well, adults needed to understand the child by studying him carefully. Lucy Sprague Mitchell's biographer explains, "At the core of the cooperative program was a single idea: rather than learning either teaching methods or specific bodies of subject matter, the teacher-in-training needed most of all to experience the excitement of learning as children could" (Antler 309). The adult would need exposure to art, literature, music, exposure to experience, with the goal of recapturing a child-like sense of the world. Into this pedagogical approach, Brown stepped and found the freedom of exploration and experimentation in which she flourished. Once a student herself, Brown found herself in Mitchell's children's literature workshop in the fall of 1935 and an author of published children's books within the next two years. In fact, within Bank Street and under the mentorship of Mitchell, Brown quickly matured as an artist, coming to take many of their techniques and "elevat[ing] Lucy's principles into poetic art" (Antler 254). Most clearly, Brown's work demonstrates her adoption of Bank Street's focus on what Mitchell called the "Here and Now," or the immediate experiences of children, in story; the school's use of children's play and language; its valorization of understanding how each childhood stage experiences reality; and its application of that understanding to encouraging child readers to grow outward from perceiving the individual to embracing the whole.

Famously, Mitchell expressed what she defined as "here and now" in the long introduction to her 1953 book of the same title, a book comprised of "experimental" children's stories that were intended to provide templates or models for stories that adult readers could mold to the individual children they cared for. Mitchell states,

> I assumed that in stories as in other educational procedure, the place to begin is the point at which the child has arrived,—to begin and lead out from. With small children this point is still within the 'here' and the 'now,' and so stories must begin with the familiar and the immediate.
>
> (*Here* 15)

For these reasons of familiarity, many of Mitchell's stories describe places, objects, sounds, and situations—such as "The Trees of the Forest" or "The Many-Horse Stable"—as opportunities for child readers to process their worlds before they were expected to move outward and to learn about places and people less immediate to their own lives. Mitchell carefully explains that she does not entirely dismiss imagination or pretend; she encourages anthropomorphism especially, but much fantasy serves only to confuse and upset young readers:

> I maintain that for the most part, myths, sagas, folk-lore depend for their significance and beauty alike upon a grasp of present social values which a young child cannot have and that our first attention should be to give him those values in terms intelligible to him.
>
> (*Here* 36)

Where could growing readers go, Mitchell might argue, if they have begun with fairy tales but cannot understand their own worlds? This focus on realism and its attempt to cull plot from everyday situations strongly describes much of Margaret Wise Brown's work as well.

Brown's *Two Little Gardeners*, for example, closely catalogues the activities of two children building, cultivating, and harvesting their garden through the spring, creating plot from enumeration of how

> the vegetables grew and they grew and they grew. Some grew so high the two little gardeners had to put up little fences for the peas to grow on, and tall poles for the beans to climb up, and sticks for the tomatoes to lean on.

As in many of both woman's stories, nothing dramatic happens, but life is lived, and time passes, and the world changes. Similarly, books like Mitchell's *A Year on the Farm* (1948) or a *Year in the City* (1948) simply recount the changes that these locations experience as the seasons change. This emphasis on children's real, lived experiences characterizes Mitchell's legacy in children's literature, a legacy in which Brown participated.

To understand the here and now lives of children, Mitchell's scientific approach to studying them centered on children's language and play. Mitchell explains,

> The new stories, like the old, have been based on direct observation of children—what they take out of the world around them and make their own in their play and in their work—and have been tried out with groups of children or with individuals. As in the old stories, children's own inimitable language has been the inspiration for whatever charm in rhythm, sound quality and pattern the new stories may have.
>
> (*Here* 9)

Through the presence of the nursery classrooms at Bank Street, Mitchell and her student teachers could directly observe and interview children themselves as they learned and played, then retreat to workshops where they wrote and shared the products of their observations. Mitchell provides throughout her introduction to *Here and Now Story Book* examples of stories told by children to demonstrate the content and form of those narratives, content and form that she then models in her own creations. For instance, Mitchell cites a story told by a two-and-a-half-year-old about an accident in the water that ends in a boat:

> I fell in water.
> Man fell in water.
> John fell in water.
> For' fell in water.
> Aunt Carrie fell in water.
>
> I pull boat out.
> Man pull boat out.
> John pull boat out.
> For' pull boat out.
> Aunt Carrie pull boat out.
> (*Here* 41)

In her own story "Marni Gets Dressed in the Morning," we can see how Mitchell uses the form and repetition of the toddler in her own stories for other child readers:

> Where water?
> Where soap?
> Where wash cloth?
> Water gone away!
> Soap gone away!
> Wash cloth gone away!
> (*Here* 60)

Mitchell highly praised: "Probably [Brown] has the most consistent and genuine interest in language of the group, perhaps of all our students. Her product, though slight, always shows sensitivity to form, sound and rhythm" (qtd. in Marcus *Margaret* 63). Brown tended to turn her rhythm and repetition into poetry or song, but there remains a strong line from the two-year-old's story, through Mitchell's writing, to such moments in Brown's narrative as, "Down the road / and down the road / and down the road / he went" (*Home for a Bunny*). This style of writing directly reflects Mitchell's and Bank Street's influence on Brown, as "I Like Dogs" does in *The Friendly Book* similarly: "I Like Dogs / Big dogs / Little dogs / Fat dogs / Doggy dogs / Old dogs /

Puppy dogs." For as Antler argues, "Lucy's focus on direct speech and the rhythmic, patterned quality of children's language as an element that should be reproduced in children's literature is probably the most enduring contribution of the 'here and now' books" (254).

In addition to observing and interviewing children with the goal of representing their language in children's books in the Bank Street School, Mitchell placed an additional emphasis on attempting to understand how each age group experiences reality. Pre-dating Piaget's work on childhood development stages, Mitchell wanted the adults at Bank Street to "unlearn" what it meant to see the world through experienced eyes and to try to adopt a child's perspective. If writers for children could accomplish this goal, then they would meet "children at their own stages of development—where they were emotionally and psychologically at that moment" (Gary 65). When an author understood where a child began in understanding, that author could then meet the child there and then gradually move outward, in what Mitchell called "relationship thinking." By this term, she meant that children, once grounded in reality, could be exposed to new ideas in ways that showed the relationships between what they already knew and the new information. It was those connections between the familiar and the unfamiliar that Mitchell believed fostered learning, understanding, and personal responsibility (*Here and Now* 25). In this way, Mitchell did not expect children to remain in the "here and now," but they would need to begin in that space in order to have something concrete from which to branch and explore. Antler understood, "Stories constructed in this way could help order the child's experiences, teaching not specific facts but how to think and understand the world" (247). This was an educational approach to teaching cognitive growth, not just direct object relations. In such Margaret Wise Brown books as *Young Kangaroo* (1959), readers can see this same philosophy at work.

Young Kangaroo is the narrative of a newly born joey whose first few months of life Brown details in what, for her, is a rather wordy book. Compared to the sentence fragments in which she often wrote, as noted above, *Young Kangaroo* might appeal to an older reader with such complex sentences as, "And to see her bounding along, clearing high bushes and fences with her long kangaroo tail streaming out behind her, no one would ever have suspected that in her pouch she harbored a little growing kangaroo" (Brown). And yet, even with twenty-two pages of text, really nothing occurs beyond description of a young kangaroo's first few months of life. It isn't until Brown anthropomorphizes the little kangaroo as his mother "threw him into a bush" during a chase by a dingo pack that any kind of climax occurs in this plot-less narrative, and only then do readers get to empathize with the protagonist momentarily as "he was alone. Alone in a bush. Silence fell about him after the dingoes had passed, and he was alone in the world," which, we are also told, is actually a common experience among kangaroos who are grown heavy enough to weigh down their mothers as they run from danger. This normal behavior among kangaroos, however, leaves the little kangaroo feeling "awful, as he had never been alone before" (Brown). She writes that he "couldn't stand it"; he "whimpered and he wailed," and he "grew tired in his grief." His mother quickly returns for him after the dingoes move on, and they are reunited, providing a conclusion to this narrative. For even this small amount of plot, however, Brown has to make the animals human-like in order for the joey to care that he has been temporarily abandoned. Mitchell writes that small children's "stories should follow their experiences. They should have no climaxes, no sense of completion" (*Here and Now* 18). This description applies to the opening of Brown's story, but as her kangaroo protagonist ages, she begins introducing relationship thinking. Beyond simply learning about kangaroos, now child readers can begin to understand their own feelings of abandonment or loneliness through the animal character in this story. Brown pulls readers into thinking that forms connections, but to do so, she has to abandon her realism just a bit to expand what her readers already understand into new ways of thinking about and processing that information.

As a direct writing teacher of Brown's, Lucy Sprague Mitchell strongly influenced Brown's writing content and form. Snippets of Brown's writing could even probably be passed off as Mitchell's writing when they sound so similarly, but as Brown matured, she took those lessons and claimed her own writing by modifying Mitchell's instructions to suit herself. She was not nearly so strict as Mitchell when it came to dismissing fantasy from children's writing, and she extended Mitchell's experimentation into areas of visual art and music. In addition, it would be remiss to claim that Brown's education at the Bank Street School was solely ordered by Lucy Sprague Mitchell when, in fact, it was the children attending the nursery school there who worked as the real instructors to both women. Though Mitchell taught Brown to study children scientifically, it was the children themselves who asked the questions, provided the feedback, related their lives, and served as the model audience for much of Brown's writing career.

Gertrude Stein

Brown's education influenced her writing through Marguerite Hearsey's and Geoffrey Chaucer's influence, and Brown's research influenced her writing through The Bank Street School, Lucy Sprague Mitchell, and child readers. Brown's reading also influenced her writing, particularly through the Modernists of her time and one of their greatest participants—Gertrude Stein. Gertrude Stein (1874–1946) remains known for launching the careers of a number of painters, such as Pablo Picasso, Juan Gris, and Henri Matisse, in addition to holding an exalted position among the writers of the Lost Generation, those such as Ernest Hemingway, F. Scott Fitzgerald, and Sherwood Anderson. With such wide interests and associations, it is no wonder that "Next to James Joyce she is the great influence on the younger literary generation, who see in her the combination of tribal wise woman and arch-priestess of aesthetic" (Porter 9). As a consummate Modernist, Stein's interest in the visual arts, music, and philosophy, as she studied psychology under William James, can be directly found in Brown's incorporation of the same disciplines into her work. Like Mitchell's and Brown's "here and now" focus, Stein valued writing that expressed space, that focused on process, that created verbal collages often devoid of plot or dialogue. Stein strove to capture what she called a "continuous present" in her texts, and all of these overlapping artistic experiments excited Brown so that when she and John McCullough wrote letters to Ernest Hemingway, Stein, and John Steinbeck in 1938, asking the famous writers to consider authoring children's books for William R. Scott publications, of which Brown served as editor, Brown was elated to hear back positively from Gertrude Stein. This partnership culminated in Stein's *The World Is Round* (1939), a story about a young female protagonist named Rose, but did not foster a relationship between Stein and Brown, to Brown's disappointment. Instead, it was McCullough, Scott's brother-in-law, who handled most of the correspondence between Stein and Scott publishers, although "In her letter [to Stein in 1940], Margaret wove a starstruck tale of admiration for the author's innovative work"

(Marcus *Margaret* 120). Even though the two women never enjoyed a personal friendship, Stein's style still shows up clearly in Brown's own writing, particularly in its use of repetition, variation, diction, sensory descriptions, expressions of reality, and its focus on American identity.

As discussed above, repetition is a central tenet of Margaret Wise Brown's writing style, and this characteristic is similarly prominent in texts by Gertrude Stein. In late 1934, Brown attended one of Stein's lectures at the Brooklyn Academy of Music and heard Stein "discuss repetition in writing as a way to reinforce understanding [...] Repetition allowed readers to grasp a basic premise, and then, by turning phrases over and over, successive layers of understanding were peeled away" (Gary 60). For instance, in her Lecture 3 from "Narration," Stein employs this technique:

> What is it that is exciting, and how can exciting be soothing if it looks like excitement and is therefore soothing or if it is exciting and is therefore soothing or if it is as if it were exciting and is therefore soothing or not soothing, all these things have to be a great deal thought about if you are to understand.
>
> (*Writings* 348)

Repetition of the terms "exciting," "soothing," and "therefore" first polarize the emotions, demonstrating their differences. Continuing their repetition and connecting those instances with "therefore" then begins to draw the terms closer together in definition and to help express the actual cause and effect relationship that they can have—excitement can actually be much more soothing than boredom. It is only by writing these words over and over again that allows our brains to begin to understand them in new ways as well as their relationships to each other.

The use of repetition has never been contained to writing:

> In 1843 Kierkegaard posited repetition as the 'modern lifeview,' the 'new category which has to be brought to light.' He was not mistaken. Writers as diverse as Nietzsche, Marx, Spengler, and Yeats explored patterns of repetition in history, while Freud established the repetition compulsion as a motive force in individual lives.
>
> (Walker 178)

Indeed, as the Modernists embraced the synesthesia of art and ideas, repetition proved a useful tool in bridging disciplines and forms. Margaret Wise Brown often used repetition to achieve a similar effect. The second and third pages of *Christmas in the Barn* (1952) use repetition to form connections between animals and their sounds: "The oxen lowed, the donkey squealed, The horses stomped, the cattle sighed." Here, the repetition is not in exact words but appears in the sentence structure. By repeating this structure four times, Brown moves the focus of these lines from which animals are present to the sounds they make, from visual signs and signifiers to auditory information. The visual presence of the words, heightened by the illustrations on each page, are then layered with the auditory sense expressed by the words, possibly also emphasized by the auditory experience of an adult reading the story aloud to a child. The repetition used by Brown fulfills a specific effect that allows these "successive layers of understanding [to be] peeled away," as Stein often intended herself (Gary 60).

Stein's use of repetition, however, rarely ended with simple reiteration. Most commonly, Stein used repetition to move her idea along progressively, bit by bit, toward a fuller understanding. Stein scholar Donald Sutherland explains that Stein "had an extraordinary mimetic faculty that allowed her to only take on the full nature of her subject [...] to follow the gradations of a theme or feeling into its farthest and faintest development" (49). In *The Making of Americans* (1925), for example, Stein writes,

> There are many kinds of men, of every kind of them there are many millions of them many millions always made to be like the others of that kind of them, of some kinds of them there are more millions made like the others of such a kind of them than there are millions made alike of some other kinds of men. Perhaps this is not really true about any kind of them, perhaps there are not less millions of one kind of men than there are millions of other kinds of them, perhaps one thinks such a thing about some kinds of men only because in some kinds of men there is more in each one of such a kind, more in the many millions of such a kind of them, of an individual feeling in every one of such a kind of men.
>
> (Qtd. in Walker 180)

Many of the words in Stein's quotation repeat, and yet progress toward an idea is still made. The first half of the idea in this excerpt moves from the individual to the group: individual kinds to millions of men to millions of kinds. Then, the idea pauses with the word "perhaps." The movement then rewinds, moving from the group back to the individual: millions of kinds to millions of men to individuals distinguished by their feelings. The repetition of diction wrestles with how two opposite states can be true at once—men can both be alike and distinctly individual at the same time. Simply stating that oxymoron would not allow the reader to follow the thought process that fully digests the idea, however, and convinces more firmly that both statements are correct.

Brown similarly employs variation by repeating words, sentence structures, or even ideas that build in minor differences in order to achieve a greater purpose. In her posthumously published *Animals in the Snow* (1995), animal friends experience "SNOW!": "Snow fell on the squirrel. / Snow fell on the bird. / Snow fell on the bunny. / Snow fell on the cat. / Snow fell on the dog. / It was snowing. / It snowed and snowed." The first stanza, consisting of the first three lines, naturally direct our attention to the animals. Since the animals on which the snow falls changes, those differences naturally pull focus. Continuing the repetition of "snow fell" into the second stanza, however, shifts reader attention to the action, as we expect by now that new animals will be introduced, and the emphasis seems to be on the snow itself. Finally, the last two lines reveal that we would be right to think more carefully about the verbs than the nouns as the page climaxes with changes in verb tense.

This page is not about the animals; it is about the snow. The minor variations in repetition here subvert readers' first impulses to prioritize the characters in the story. Only by saying it over and over again does Brown teach us that she wants us to ponder the snow itself. For both Stein and Brown, the use of repetition achieves a higher purpose, even higher than emphasizing, as many poets intend with repetition. Instead, it conveys an idea, a truth, with simplicity.

Gertrude Stein's apparent simplicity but actual depth was one of the characteristics that drew William Scott publishers to consider her as a possible children's author. In fact, the Bank Street Writers Laboratory's Wednesday night workshopping groups studied Stein before the publishing company formed. They found Stein's writing

> especially pertinent. The inherent playfulness of her verse and prose, her exuberant manner of cadenced repetition (and of subtle

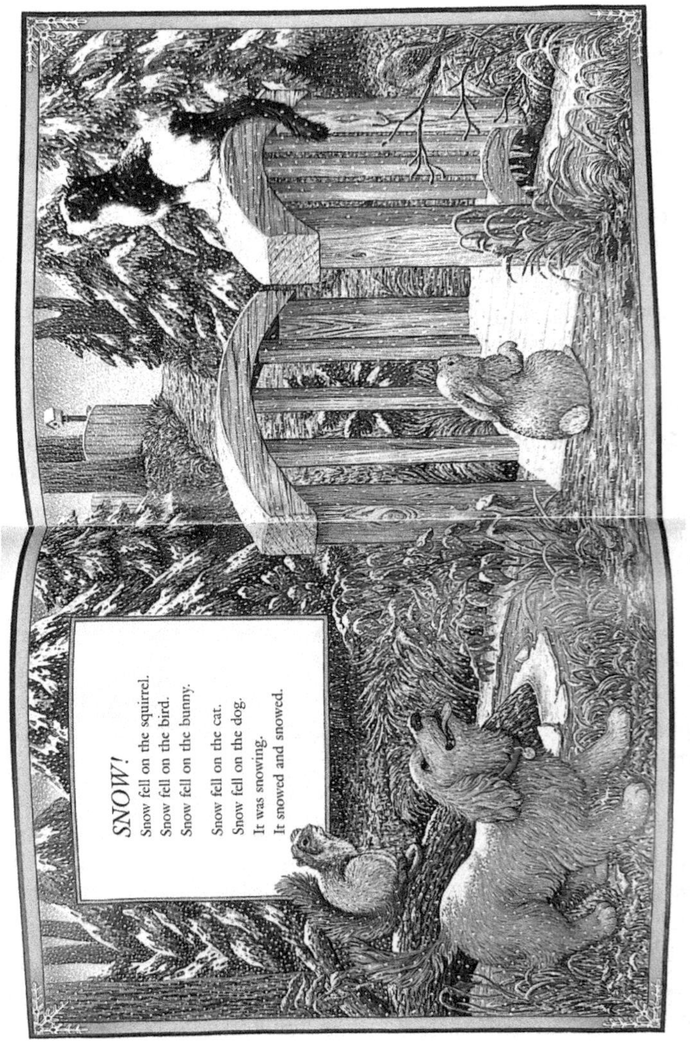

Figure 1.3 Brown, Margaret Wise. *Animals in the Snow*. Hyperion, 1995. pp. 3–4.

> variation within repetition), and her peculiar genius for making words seem to speak directly from the page were all elements of attitude and style that Margaret and the others were eager to incorporate into their own work.
>
> (Marcus *Margaret* 86)

Just as these aspiring writers had found children's books an ideal playground for experimentation and for returning to the basics of the English language, so they saw Gertrude Stein making similar moves in her own writing, particularly in her diction. Centrally, Stein played with words in an attempt to disassociate them from their conventional meanings. Releasing them from the associations, shades of meaning, context, and biases they had accumulated like barnacles on a whale could free them to express fresh truths. Writer William H. Gass explains that,

> Words, of course, were tender buttons, to be sorted and played with, admired and arranged, and she felt that language in English literature had become increasingly stiff and resistant, and that words had to be pried out of their formulas, freed, and allowed to regain their former Elizabethan fluidity."
>
> (158)

Just as when we repeat a word or a name to exhaustion it can lose its familiarity and sound like nonsense, so does Stein often repeat or choose words with the intention of disengaging them from normalcy in order to rediscover their possibilities. She explained in a lecture to students,

> Now listen! Can't you see that when the language was new—as it was with Chaucer and Homer—the poet could use the name of a thing and the thing was really there? He could say 'O moon,' 'O sea,' 'O love' and the moon and the sea and love were really there. And can't you see that after hundreds of years had gone by and thousands of poems had been written, he could call on those words and find that they were just worn out literary words? The excitingness of pure being had withdrawn from them; they were just rather stale literary words. Now the poet has to work in the excitingness of pure being; he has to get back that intensity into the language.
>
> (Qtd. in Wilder v–vi)

How can writers make the English language new? Gertrude Stein argues that by separating words from their expected meanings, by repeating words until they sound like nonsense, by creating oxymorons that are possible, by playing with words in unexpected ways, writers can help readers think along fresh paths. Renewing language is to renew thought.

Margaret Wise Brown attempts this purpose on a different level for children whose minds are already fresher, but Stein's playfulness with the intent to redirect thought is still present in most of her works. In *The Sleepy ABC Book* (1953), illustrated by Esphyr Slobodkina, for instance, each page features a letter of the alphabet with a brief line that uses the letter to describe the bedtime process. Most of these lines are comforting: "G is for Grazing of sleepy sheep / H is for Heaven high over head." But just a few times through the book, an unexpected line follows its letter, letters such as "I is for me who is going to bed." The letter "I" certainly does not begin the word "me," but the meaning of the word "I" does refer to the same object as "me." Between H and I, Brown moves from referencing letters to referencing the meaning of the words those letters spell. Playing with the words in this way causes readers to see new truths they may not have expected. Similarly, following N, Brown writes, "O is for 'Oh!' at the story they read." Here, the letter O stands both as the first letter in the word "Oh" and the sound that the letter makes. Brown shows the many different ways that language can work in this simple ABC book. Her most experimental letter in this book, and the letter that often gives authors of ABC books pause, is X. She writes, "X is for all of the things you can play." Here, it takes quite a bit of guessing to understand how the letter X is related to different games that children play, but that guessing is yet another facet of language. Maybe X might show up if children crossed off ideas of games on a list. Maybe X represents game tiles or pieces. Maybe X refers to specific games, like X Marks the Spot.

The illustrations do not give much indication of intended meaning as they picture a child dressed as a Native American, a child dressed as a cowboy, and a child riding a rocking horse. But X is already a mystery letter, difficult to sound out and used sparingly; Brown's description of its uses remains just as elusive. While Brown's diction does not go quite as far as Stein's in completely disassociating words from their conventional meanings, she does seem to use words in multiple ways to keep readers guessing, surprised, and thinking about what words are and how language communicates.

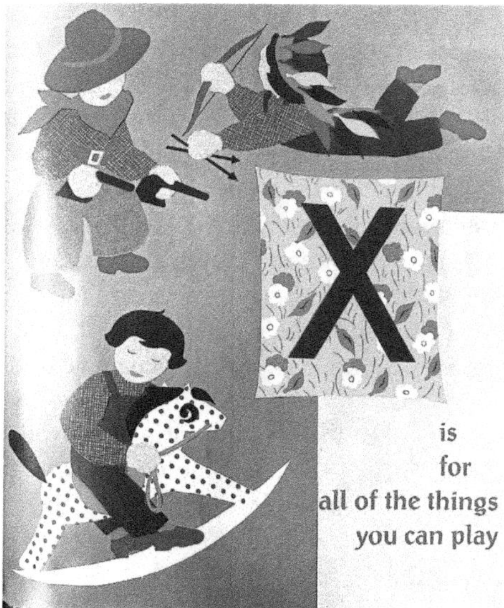

Figure 1.4 Brown, Margaret Wise. *The Sleepy ABC Book*. Lothrop, Lee & Shepard Co., 1953. p. 28.

Gertrude Stein's and Margaret Wise Brown's deep dive into language and its meaning often took them into sensory impressions. In fact, this effect is what Sherwood Anderson noted about Stein's writing when he reported, "[Stein] is laying word against word, relating sound to sound, feeling for the taste, the smell, the rhythm of the individual word" (8). Repetition and variation could certainly lead readers into a more physical experience of the words Stein commonly used, especially when their understanding is more readily accessed by reading her texts aloud. But Stein also wrote inherently sensory descriptions, as seen in her three-page novel, *What Does She See When She Shuts Her Eyes* (1936):

> When she shuts her eyes she sees the green things among which she has been working and then as she falls asleep she sees them be a little different. The green things then have black roots and the black roots have red stems and then she is exhausted.
>
> (*Writings* 491)

Sight remains the most explicit sense accessed here, with the list of plants and their colors, but touch and even proprioception enter Stein's description by the end. The roots, described as black, connotes soil and its thick, damp, mustiness. Stein's inclusion of her character "working" these plants, sleeping, and then feeling "exhausted" also conjures the sense of bodily awareness, a reader's empathy of sensation that we have all experienced in working outdoors. This predilection in description suited Stein for writing children's texts at the same time that it contributed to her role as a Modernist: "The modernist aesthetic of recreating in art the immediacy of sensory impressions seemed to coincide with young children's natural reliance on their senses as the primary means of both experiencing and expressing themselves about the world" (Marcus *Margaret* 86). Certainly, Stein's sensory descriptions similarly describe Brown's writing as well.

In one of my favorites of Brown's poems, published as the titular poem in her 2002 collection *Give Yourself to the Rain*, Brown writes,

> Give yourself to the rain when it falls
> Give yourself to the wind
> Go with it
> Blow through the bright dark
> Green light on trees
> Listen to the rain
> Again—through sleep
> Dream of it
> Brace nothing against it
> Safe in your bed
> Listen
> And give yourself to the rain
> When it falls down.

The poem begins with visual and tactile sensory descriptions: the rain—wet, falling, wind, blowing. Then more visual imagery appears in the "bright dark" oxymoron of light-colored rain from a dark sky among green trees. Next follows the auditory command to "listen" to the rain, its sound on house and plant. Interestingly, Brown's next line takes us back to Stein's dreaming character when she urges readers to "Dream of it," and ends with a similar proprioceptive encouragement to relax, "Brace nothing," and "give yourself" to the full sensory experience of rain. Descriptions abound in most of Brown's writing, primarily attributable to her young audience, but possibly also grounded in a modern aesthetic, markedly different from more contemporary writers such as Sandra Boynton or Mo Willems whose texts rely more heavily on nonsense, characters, and plot. Part of the intent behind these sensory-laden narratives could be Brown's, and Stein's, interest in expressing perceptions of reality.

Lucy Sprague Mitchell valued verbalizing a child's reality, an experience of the world. Gertrude Stein similarly valued analyzing "the given in ordinary human experience with full awareness of its mystery. She raises questions as to the nature of perception, the meaning of being, the boundlessness of space and the roundness of the world, the passage of time and the nature of personality and identity, and the activities of genius" (Stewart 69). The human presence in personal and collective experience as well as our conflation of inner and outer awareness of those states of being preoccupy both Stein and Brown in their authorships. For Stein, reality included activity, sensory perceptions, thoughts and analysis of those experiences, interruptions of experience, rewritings of personal narratives, estrangement from normalcy, all seen in her writing. In fact, much of her writing strives to recreate these situations in art, much did as the impressionist painters she knew and the philosophers and psychologists with whom she worked and played. In her lecture "Pictures," Stein explains,

> Once the *Little Review* had a questionnaire, it was for their farewell number, and they asked everybody whose work they had printed to answer a number of questions. One of the questions was, what do you feel about modern art. I answered, I like to look at it. That was my real answer because I do, I do like to look at it, that is at the picture part of modern art. The other parts of it interest me much less. (*Writings* 224)

For some, this kind of answer could represent a dismissal of the question, a shrug. For others, the simplicity of the answer could seem not thoughtful enough. For Gertrude Stein, she expresses her reality, her truth, and expects readers to consider the depth in her pithiness. If it is real, for Stein, and it is true, it can be art.

Brown too has a gift for facing experience and relating it simply and directly, especially the remembered experience of childhood. Brown explained that memory was "the ultimate source of her creative work," and she particularly focused on those childhood states of being that were commonly felt, realizing that "if she could write about the common threads of childhood in her own books, then maybe they, like fables, would last" (Marcus *Margaret* 7; Gary 120). Brown's 1958 *The Dead Bird*, for example, still stands as one of the best expressions of childhood encounters with death that children's literature offers. In this story, a group of four children find a dead bird and confront death both physically and metaphysically. Brown recounts this life truth by using sensory descriptions, "it had not been dead for long—it was still warm and its eyes were closed," by using repetition of the word "dead" twelve times, and by recounting the reality of traditions surrounding death: "They could have a funeral and sing to it the way grown-up people did when someone died." The children bury the bird, sing a song to it, pick flowers for the grave, and then eventually "forgot," ending with a picture of them playing in a field as the grave of the bird remains hidden among the trees, no longer the children's priority—a truth about death. The book uses simple, direct diction and faces a very difficult topic straight on, without apology or embarrassment, expressing reality for many children and adults.

Artists of overlapping time periods, Gertrude Stein and Margaret Wise Brown wrote pieces that still have much in common. While Stein never directly instructed Brown in writing, Brown certainly saw Stein as a teacher and mentor, and many of Stein's experimental characteristics surface in Brown's stories, keeping them fresh and timely more than half a century later. Thornton Wilder once stated, "for Miss Stein all intellectual activities—philosophical speculation, literary criticism, narration—had to be refreshed at the source," and this raw, natural newness continues to describe Brown's writing as well (26). In her article "Creative Writing for Children," published in the 1951 *The Book of Knowledge Annual*, Brown states, "I am grateful to the world of children's books for remaining one of the purest and freest fields for experimental writing today" (81).

Margaret Wise Brown stories retain a unique writing style characterized by repetition, rhythm, a musicality of phrasing, listing, and combining genres of prose and poetry. In addition to her own genius, Brown's style developed from such direct and indirect influences as Geoffrey Chaucer, Lucy Sprague Mitchell and the child students at the Bank Street School, and such Modernists as Gertrude Stein. Her scientific approach to art and yet value of language and expression culminated in a literary legacy that far exceeds her lifetime. Leonard Marcus concludes,

> Margaret also occupied a unique place as an inspired author for the very youngest, a group of children for whom few had even thought to write before; and no author before or since has managed so well to shape books that complete what Margaret herself once called the 'natural impulse to amuse and to delight and comfort' small children.
>
> (*Margaret* 2)

Brown's combination of the past and the new in technique, philosophy, theme, and perspective resulted in a beautiful oeuvre spanning readerships, time, and topic.

Notes

1 More books of Brown's have been published since her death, but those did not start appearing in earnest until the turn of the twenty-first century and still count for only a small percentage of her oeuvre.

2 Defining poetry in Margaret Wise Brown's stories is subjective and certainly includes the other aspects of her style discussed in this chapter: her phrasing, her rhythm and pattern, and the repetition she employs. However, those aspects can exist independently of the poetic moments in her stories, and the poetry she writes often stands alone as moments within the greater stylistic narratives. Brown's poetic moments may also include alliteration, anaphora, assonance and consonance, and, of course, rhyme. For these reasons, it's useful to discuss Brown's poetry as a separate aspect of her writing style, although there certainly remains overlap and fluidity between each of these forms.

3 Most definitions of "prose poem," such as *The Poetry Foundation*'s and *The Oxford English Dictionary*'s, describe this genre as prose which contains a high number of literary elements more commonly found in poetry, such as concentrated figures of speech, rhyme, and even subtle rhythms.

4 A good place to begin a study of the musical nature of Chaucer's *Tales* is Michael Erik Bigley's *Musicality, Subjectivity, and the Canterbury Tales*, 2007.

5 Unless the diction of Chaucer's original Middle English is important for the specific claim or selection, quotations from *The Canterbury Tales* will appear in translated form, in Modern English, to prioritize clarity for the readers of this project who may not be Chaucer or Middle English scholars.

6 Some sources list Mitchell's tenure at Bank Street beginning as early as 1916 because it marks the year she began working for the Bureau of Educational Experiments. However, the actual Bank Street School, as we now know it, was not built until 1930. Margaret Wise Brown knew Mitchell

in the context of Bank Street, so the 1930 date remains more pertinent for a discussion of the relationship between these two women. Lucy Sprague Mitchell, ever the champion of equality, would also have disliked the terms "ran" or "led" in reference to her position at Bank Street, but for all practical purposes, since her role defined her as the leader or head of the school, I will use these terms abashedly with muttered apology to Lucy herself.

References

Anderson, Sherwood. "An American Impression." *Modern Critical Views: Gertrude Stein*, edited by Harold Bloom. Chelsea House, 1986, pp. 7–8.

Antler, Joyce. *Lucy Sprague Mitchell: The Making of A Modern Woman*. Yale UP, 1987.

Badar, Barbara. *American Picture Books from Noah's Ark to the Beast Within*. Macmillan, 1976.

Brown, Margaret Wise. *A Child's Goodnight Book*. Addison-Wesley, 1943.

———. *Animals in the Snow*. Hyperion, 1995.

———. *Christmas in the Barn*. Thomas Y. Crowell, 1952.

———. "Creative Writing for Children." *The Book of Knowledge Annual: 1951*, edited by E.V. McLoughlin. The Grolier Society, 1951, pp. 77–81.

———. *Give Yourself to the Rain*. Margaret K. McElderry Books, 2002.

———. *Home for a Bunny*, illustrated by Garth Williams. Golden Books, 1956.

———. *The Color Kittens*. Golden Books, 1949.

———. *The Dead Bird*. HarperCollins, 1958.

———. *The Friendly Book*. Golden Books, 1954.

———. *The Little Fisherman*. William R. Scott, 1945.

———. *The Runaway Bunny*, illustrated by Clement Hurd. Harper, 1942.

———. *The Sleepy ABC Book*. Lothrop, Lee & Shepard Co., 1953.

———. *The Wonderful House*. Golden Books, 1950.

———. *Two Little Gardeners*. Golden Books, 1951.

———. *Under the Sun and the Moon and Other Poems*. Hyperion, 1993.

———. *Young Kangaroo*. The World's Work, 1959.

Chaucer, Geoffrey. *The Canterbury Tales*, translated by R.M. Lumiansky. Simon & Schuster, 2001.

Conrad, JoAnn. "Modernity and Modernism in Twentieth-Century American Picturebooks." *International Research in Children's Literature*, 12, 2, December 2019, pp. 127–53.

David, Alfred, M.H. Abrams & Stephen Greenblatt, editors. "Geoffrey Chaucer (ca. 1343–1400)." *The Norton Anthology of English Literature: The Middle Ages*, 7th ed, vol. 1A. W.W. Norton and Company, 2000, pp. 210–316.

Gary, Amy. *In the Great Green Room: The Brilliant and Bold Life of Margaret Wise Brown*. Flatiron, 2016.

Gass, William H. "Gertrude Stein and the Geography of the Sentence: 'Tender Buttons.'" *Modern Critical Views: Gertrude Stein*, edited by Harold Bloom. Chelsea House, 1986, pp. 145–63.

Lumiansky, R.M. "Some Introductory Observations for the Modern Reader of The Canterbury Tales." *The Canterbury Tales*, translated by Lumiansky. Simon & Schuster, 2001, pp. xxi–xxxix.

Marcus, Leonard S. *Margaret Wise Brown: Awakened by the Moon*. Beacon, 1992.

———. "Margaret Wise Brown." *Dictionary of Literary Biography: American Writers for Children, 1900–1960*, edited by John Cech, vol. 22. Bruccoli Clark, 1983, pp. 42–70.

Mitchell, Lucy Sprague. *A Year in the City*. Simon & Schuster, 1948.

———. *A Year on the Farm*. Simon & Schuster, 1948.

———. *Two Lives: The Story of Wesley Clair Mitchell and Myself*. Simon & Schuster, 1953.

Mitchell, Lucy Sprague. *Here and Now Story Book*. Dover Publications, 2015.

Munden, Paul. "Playing with Time: Prose Poetry and the Elastic Moment." *Text: Journal of Writing and Writing Courses*, 46, October 2017, pp. 1–13.

Pearsall, Derek, editor. "Geoffrey Chaucer (*c*. 1343–1400)." *Chaucer to Spenser: An Anthology of Writings in English 1375–1575*. Blackwell, 1999, pp. 1–181.

Phillips, Susan E. "Chaucer's Language Lessons." *The Chaucer Review*, 46, 1 & 2, 2011, pp. 39–59.

Piaget, Jean. *The Language and Thought of the Child*. 1928, Routledge, 2001.

Porter, Katherine Anne. "Everybody Is a Real One." *Modern Critical Views: Gertrude Stein*, edited by Harold Bloom. Chelsea House, 1986, pp. 9–12.

Stanton, Joseph. "Goodnight Nobody: Comfort and the Vast Dark in the Poems of Margaret Wise Brown and her Collaborators." *The Important Book: Children's Picture Books as Art and Literature*. Scarecrow, 2005, pp. 7–17.

Stein, Gertrude. *Writings 1932–1946*, edited by Catherine R. Stimpson & Harriet Chessman. The Library of America, 1998.

Stewart, Allegra. "The Quality of Gertrude Stein's Creativity." *Modern Critical Views: Gertrude Stein*, edited by Harold Bloom. Chelsea House, 1986, pp. 65–79.

Susina, Jan. "Children's Reading, Repetition, and Rereading: Gertrude Stein, Margaret Wise Brown, and Goodnight Moon." *Second Thoughts: A Focus on Rereading*, edited by David Galef. Wayne State UP, 1998, pp. 115–25.

Sutherland, Donald. "Three Lives." *Modern Critical Views: Gertrude Stein*, edited by Harold Bloom. Chelsea House, 1986, pp. 47–63.

Walker, Jayne L. "History as Repetition: 'The Making of Americans.'" *Modern Critical Views: Gertrude Stein*, edited by Harold Bloom. Chelsea House, 1986, pp. 177–99.

Wilder, Thornton. "Introduction. Gertrude Stein: *Four in America.*" Yale UP, 1947, pp. v–xxvi.

Williams, David. "General Introduction: *The Canterbury Tales* and the Tradition of English Literature." *The Canterbury Tales*, translated by R.M. Lumiansky. Simon & Schuster, 1990, pp. xiii–xx.

2 The Visual Artist

Just as Margaret Wise Brown's oeuvre reflects the tenets of Modernism, a time and philosophy in which she purposefully participated, so too did her personal perspectives of the world express some of the avant-garde values of the movement. The impact occurred in both directions. Brown's outlook on life and reality, coinciding with the Modernist movement, led to books that merged multiple artistic genres, one of the most significant blendings remaining writing and visual art. Children's picture books naturally blend the two mediums, but only certain authors, among those the ones who even have a voice in the choosing of their books' illustrators, reach beyond illustrations that depict the mood or theme of their words. Margaret Wise Brown remains a central figure among children's picture book authors who sought not only to represent her stories well visually in a thoughtful manner, but to offer child readers two genuine mediums of high art—literary and visual art.

In her article on Brown's feline characters, Suzanne Rahn comments,

> In the cottage she built for Michael Strange, an ornate antique frame was hung to outline not a painting but a window looking out onto a dark forest of spruces […] This Picture Window, as Brown called it, an exact reversal of the Hundred Windows [in her *The House of a Hundred Windows*], raises the same speculations about the power of the frame, and the relation of art to reality.
>
> (Rahn 158)

As Rahn notices, Brown both saw and created visual art out of her own realities. Brown saw art existing all around her in the man-made

DOI: 10.4324/9781032727028-3

and natural worlds, and by hanging literal and metaphorical frames, she helped others recognize that art as well. Certainly, one method of revealing that visual art to children would be to illustrate her own picture books, as Leonard Marcus posits she would have done "had she been capable of doing so" ("Seen" 200). Brown's personal artistic skill set, however, remained in working with words, not paints and pencils:

> Margaret also thought about studying painting, but after one uninspiring session at the Art Students League she decided 'to get a pile of green vegetables and paint by myself at home instead of paying to paint a pile of naked figures'.
>
> (Marcus *Margaret* 41)

Her turn from visual art to literary art did nothing to compromise her ability to recognize the talent of other illustrators and painters when she saw it, however.

In her respect for the genre of children's literature, and in her recognition of the potential it held, Brown believed picture books offered a medium of opportunity for both child readers and visual artists. Brown was not alone in this belief as the American Library Association awarded the first Caldecott Medal for illustrations in children's books in 1938 to Dorothy P. Lathrop for her work on *Animals of the Bible, A Picture Book*, a year after Brown published her own first book, *When the Wind Blew*, in 1937. The presence of the award

> lent added prestige to the picture book as an art form just as a growing number of American illustrators were turning to the genre as an outlet for their talents and an influx of European émigré artists was further enriching the scene.
>
> (Marcus *Golden* 30)

This appreciation for picture book illustrations was not new, as some of the nicest children's books at the time were intended to expose children to visual art; their high cost reflected the intended seriousness of these purchases and the dual audiences of both child and adult (Marcus *Golden* 32). The power of art to represent internal worlds spoke clearly to Brown, and the possibilities afforded by visual art were ideas she wanted to share with children. Lucy Sprague Mitchell remembered of her mentorship with Brown that a remark she had made "suddenly opened up [for Brown] the possibility of giving back to children the realities in their own world, not with photographic literalness, but magically heightened" (Mitchell "Margaret" 19). Visual art could provide child readers with reflections of their own minds, mirrors that echoed their worlds in fantastic ways. While many of Brown's texts demonstrate Bank Street's here and now themes, from parental schedules to relationships between objects, Brown also incorporated flavors of fantasy by anthropomorphizing animal characters and imagining unknowable worlds. The art she chose to depict such stories similarly reflected the natural combinations of reality and fantasy experienced by imaginative children.

Children were certainly Brown's target audience, but another important impetus for the artwork in her children's picture books was her interest in showcasing the artistic talent of new illustrators. In many ways, Margaret Wise Brown served as a "curator" of visual art, using her books as art collections for new illustrators. Many of these new illustrators were traveling to America in the late 1930s, along with other artists, writers, and intellectuals, to escape Hitler's threat in Europe (Marcus *Golden* 37). In meeting newly arrived talent through friends or activities in New York City, Brown encouraged these artists to illustrate books she worked on and, at times, she specifically wrote texts with particular illustrators in mind. Brown respected these artists, such illustrators as Ilya Bolotowsky, Jean Charlot, Tibor Gergely, and Esphyr Slobodkina: "At a time when illustrators were often paid a flat fee for their services and authors received all the royalties from a book, Margaret routinely insisted on equal payment for her collaborators" (Marcus *Margaret* 223). Brown worked to offer real art to her readers, to nurture the growing field of children's literature, and to encourage talent when she saw it. Although most of the artists with whom Brown collaborated found additional success independently from her support, both Brown's books and new illustrators' careers benefited from the partnership.

Upon reviewing Margaret Wise Brown's body of work, many readers are struck by its variety of illustrations. William Scott, an early publisher of Brown's books, commented that she "collected" artists, and this habit certainly contributed to diverse artwork for her stories (Marcus "Margaret" 60). In addition to the number of artists working to illustrate her books, however, were the Modernist tendencies of many of these artists to experiment with multiple artistic styles themselves. Leonard Weisgard, particularly his work in Brown's *The*

Important Book, is widely hailed for his impressive contributions to avant-garde picture book art, and Esphyr Slobodkina is recognized for introducing Constructivism:

> Constructivism was the kinetic Russian Revolution-era graphic explosion that set out, originally, to educate the unlettered Soviet masses (children included) by means of highly distilled, semi-abstract geometric images that could be "read" at a glance. Russian emigrée artist Esphyr Slobodkina introduced Constructivism to the American picture book with her dazzling collage illustrations for Margaret Wise Brown's *The Little Fireman* (1938).
>
> (Marcus "Back" 39)

Brown viewed her collaborations as productive for all involved, from reader to writer, illustrator to publisher, and the experimental nature of her products supported her Modernist interests. A close analysis of Brown's work with three of her most common artistic partners, Leonard Weisgard, Clement Hurd, and Garth Williams, demonstrates her desire to introduce children to new ideas and new perspectives through both text and illustration.[1]

Leonard Weisgard

When Margaret Wise Brown met Leonard Weisgard in 1938, he was a tall twenty-three-year-old interviewing for the job of illustrating Brown's *The World Is Round.* He had begun his career as a magazine illustrator but went on to become "one of the most prolific American illustrators of the twentieth century," working on more than two hundred books (Salisbury 71). With Brown alone, Weisgard contributed to more than twenty picture books. Individually, Weisgard is "known for his embrace of modernism," a style of his "which owed something to Russian Constructivism, McKnight Kauffer's modernist graphics, and Stuart Davis's cubist phase" (Marcus "Shape" 9; Marcus *Margaret* 109). Weisgard proved adept at shifting his artistic style to reflect theme, demonstrating his many talents with a variety of mediums.

Weisgard was Brown's most frequent collaborator, and one explanation for their combined success is the similar goals they desired to achieve through picture books:

> Working closely together, Weisgard and Brown approached the picture book as an synesthetic art form: an opportunity to combine

> words and images in such a way as to amplify the expressive power of both media, thereby creating an intensely immediate sensory experience for children that was greater than the sum of its parts.
> (Marcus "Seen" 201)

The pair's *Noisy Book* series remains one of their clearest and most representative collaborations. The *Noisy Books* came about as a challenge for Brown and Weisgard regarding their interest in representing sound through image, "a Symbolist-related speculation of Weisgard's that sounds might be translated into visual equivalents through the colors and shapes of an illustration" (Marcus *Margaret* 110). In their *Seashore Noisy Book* (1941), for example, the book opens with the sounds that seagulls make "flying in the air." The birds themselves appear just above the text, represented by disconnected, blurred lines or brush strokes that end in sharp angles, just as the sound, "scree scree scree," with its voiceless velar stop in the "c" and the "ee" diphthong, communicates an angularity, a harshness that mirrors the illustration. Similarly, near the center of the picture book appear two black and white pages depicting a black ocean, sky, and boat with a white moon, horizon, and faint outlining of the boat and rippling water. The text reads, "It was night and Muffin didn't hear a thing but the gentle lapping waves around the boat." On these pages, the absence of color and objects represents absence of sound. The great darkness of the pages in contrast to the small, soft, white ripples of water communicate the smallness of sound compared to the vastness of space. Weisgard explains in his 1947 Caldecott Medal speech that

> we experimented with color for sound and shapes for emotion, letting the child bring the magic of movement, in a series of *Noisy* books. So that a radiator would be placed in a shape suggested by the hissing noise it makes, and the round sound of a ticking clock would put it into a circle.

Indeed, at times the illustrations in this picture book change from more realistic scene portrayal to sensory impressions. When the text catalogues lobsters crawling, a shark, a swordfish, and little tiny fish swimming, the accompanying picture uses color and shape to gesture toward images that these words may bring to mind, rather than attempting realistic images of these subjects.

The Seashore Noisy Book goes beyond its collaborators' initial goals of representing sound through image, however. The *Noisy Books* serve as metafictive picture books as they point to the constructedness of words and pictures in dialogue with both each other and with readers. When Brown writes that "Muffin could hear: / Whoooo / Whoooo / Whoooo / Whoooo / What was that? / And he could hear: / lapping slapping / slap lap lap / against the side of the boat. / What was that?" the text's tiered, stepped physical placement on the page creates an illustration of its own, mimicking the prow of the sailboat at the bottom of the page and the jutting cliffs illustrated on the facing page.

Here, Brown's text illustrates the narrative while Weisgard's illustrations depict the sounds of the text. This intimate collaboration permits a transparency of construction as each medium helps carry some of the narrative burden of its partner. It also challenges reader assumptions that words exercise certain functions and that illustrations do different work.

The use of text as part of illustrations appears in many picture books; Brown and Weisgard join authors and illustrators such as Virginia Lee Burton who are famous for deeply incorporated text placement that actually contributes to parts of the image itself. Some of Brown and Weisgard's *Noisy Books* separate text on one page and illustration on an opposing page, but others continue experimenting with "visual markings for language actually becom[ing] part of the depicted scene" (Nodelman 55). In *The Summer Noisy Book* (1951), for example, an illustration reaches over both pages in an early two-page spread to show Muffin looking out the back window of a car, the curvy road extending in front of the car. The words appear in the same color as the grass that covers a significant portion of both pages and extends in a curvy form down the road that Muffin's car is about to drive up. This placement of text does not create a form itself, but as readers' eyes scan the words from the top of the left page down and examine the illustration, whose directed tension moves from the bottom of the right page, up to the top of the left page, the two artistic mediums meet each other in the middle, balanced and conciliatory. Such pages demonstrate cooperation of the two artists and their mediums in highly successful ways. Similarly, on a later page, the words "It was a cat" appear in a yellow banner at the top of the page, and the words "and seven little kittens" stand in a red banner at the bottom of the page, separated by an illustration of a mother cat and seven kittens. Here again, the words and illustrations take turns demanding reader attention. This collaboration between artistic forms

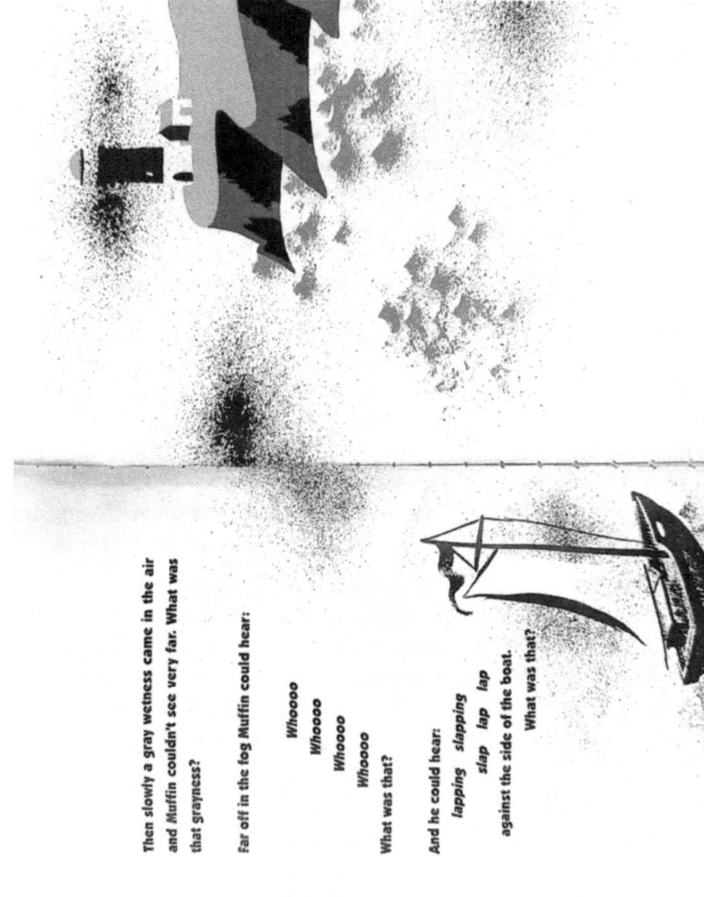

Figure 2.1 Brown, Margaret Wise. *The Seashore Noisy Book*. HarperCollins, 1941. p. 2.

amplifies the impact of each individually and offers an admirable, Modern, artistic project for a child audience:

> The seven Noisy volumes that Brown and Weisgard did see through to publication (and an eighth volume, *The Winter Noisy Book*, illustrated in 1947 by Charles G. Shaw) represent an important cultural legacy as the books which, more than any others, introduced the spirit of modernism into American writing and illustration for children. Heeding the modernist imperative to "make it new," Brown, Weisgard, and their like-mined colleagues succeeded in bringing kinetic language, stylized abstraction, and an urgent immediacy to the words and pictures of books intended for people for whom the world itself was a brand new experience.
>
> (Marcus "Seen" 202)

The books written and illustrated by these two friends move beyond achieved cooperation and collaboration, however. Some of their texts also explore weighty topics of personal perspective and the individual's relationship to self, as *The Little Island* (1946) and *The Important Book* (1949) demonstrate.

When Weisgard won the 1948 Caldecott Medal for *The Little Island*, written by Brown, a different, more realistic painting style of his earned applause. Leonard Marcus recognizes that "Weisgard recalibrated his illustration style to suit each new manuscript, revealing equal finesse at executing busy crowd scenes and elaborate decorative patterns, or simply catching the essence of a character in a few telling lines" ("Shape" 20). In this story about a small island and the wildlife that enjoys it, such paintings as Weisgard's silhouette of kingfishers and a close-up of lobsters have received great praise for their color, line, and realism. Even within this less experimental style, however, Weisgard incorporates moments of Surrealism that encourage readers to consider personal identity.

This award-winning picture book teaches that the value of the individual is not created by others but the presence and relation of the individual to oneself determines self-value. For instance, the seasons themselves are created by the Island and what happens on it: "Small flowers, white and blue, / and violets with golden eyes / and little waxy white-pink chuckleberry blossoms / and one tickly smelling pear tree / bloomed on the Island. / And that was the spring." The way that Brown chooses to describe what the Island produces before defining the production as a particular season gives the Island agency, rather than portraying it at the mercy of larger forces. In other pages, Brown describes additional changes, such as Summer or night, as visitors: "the seals came […] the kingfishers came […] Summer had come to the little Island […] Birds came […] Night came […] Then came the storm […] Autumn came […] Winter came […] Nights and days came and passed." Each visitor arrives and later leaves, emphasized by the repeated refrain throughout the picture book. By reinforcing the temporary state of each visitor, Brown again portrays the Island as the constant, the self-possessed, reliable presence that provides others with refuge. The Island is not defined by external situations; it remains.

Both narratively and visually, however, the little Island is also quickly defined as a space of connection and relationship. The first two-page spread reads, "There was a little Island in the ocean. / Around it the winds blew / And the birds flew / And the tides rose and fell on the shore." The text, appearing on the left-hand page, describes the island amid both sky and water, a bridge between the two spaces. On the right-hand page, the Island itself appears, rising vertically from a sea in which horizontal waves break and reach into a sky in which horizontal clouds blow.

The lines and colors of the image intensify the theme: this Island is small in a vast emptiness, but even in its smallness, it binds. Similarly, while the text appears on one page and the colored image remains separate on another, black and white images leak over onto the text's page, connecting the two disparate mediums. The narrative continues this theme of connection as the Island draws both sea creatures and birds, providing a center. Here, relationship can often make defining characteristics clearer, and *The Little Island* values contrast.

The central event of the picture book strengthens Brown and Weisgard's point. Appearing right in the middle of the story, a little kitten arrives on the Island with people who visit for a picnic. With the kitten's arrival, the Island speaks for the first time, and the two characters, "child surrogates," have a conversation about connection and difference (Stanton "Goodnight" 14). This conversation leads to a moment of Surrealism in which the kitten leaps into the air, wondering, "Maybe I am a little Island too […] a little fur Island in the air."

Weisgard illustrates this moment with the kitten levitating far above the trees and flying seagulls, the cat's body crossing the horizon to connect sky and sea. The kitten does not look happy or free, however,

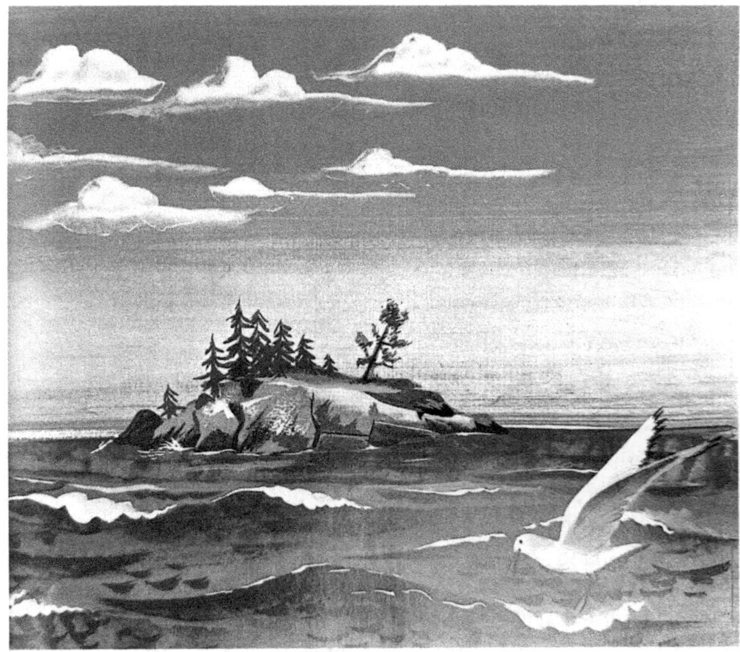

Figure 2.2 Brown, Margaret Wise. *The Little Island.* Doubleday, 1946. p. 2.

and his eyes remain focused on the land beneath him. The kitten tells the Island that he is a part of the "big world," a definition he seems to prefer over the possibility of being a fur island, and he claims that the little Island is cut off "from the land." In this discussion, the kitten valorizes connection over individuality; since the Island, apparently, is not connected to land, the kitten perceives it as isolated and, therefore, lacking. What he soon learns though is that the little Island is connected to the land beneath the water, and the book ends with the lesson that both individuality and connection through relationship provide wholeness: "And it was good to be a little Island. / A part of the world / and a world of its own." In this way, the Island (and the individual child) nurtures life, remains mysterious, and allows for exploration and curiosity as it provides a constant in its self-assured identity. It is only through experiencing both Brown's text and Weisgard's pictures together that this message is clearly expressed, a similar message to that made by *The Important Book.*

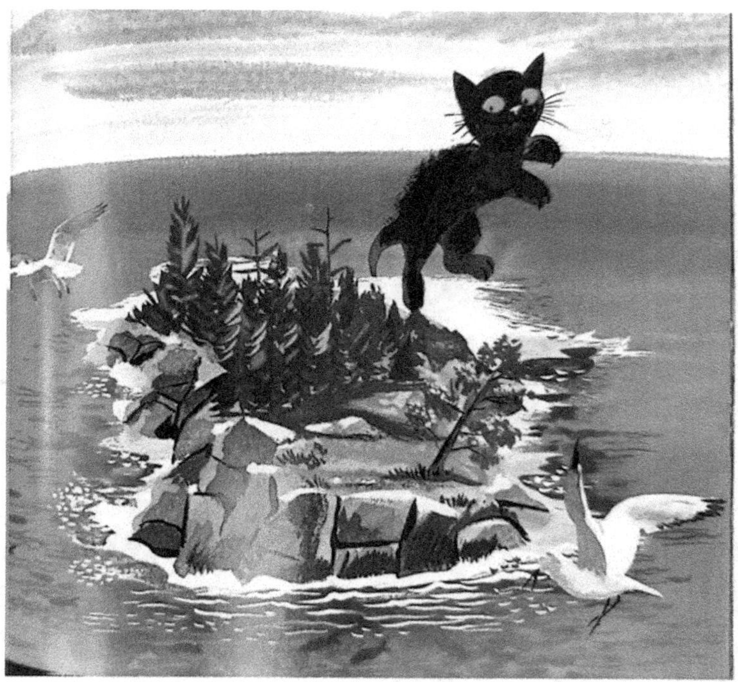

Figure 2.3 Brown, Margaret Wise. *The Little Island*. Doubleday, 1946. p. 24.

The Important Book (1949) has certainly received the most critical and scholarly attention among Brown's books for its challenge to the traditional tenets of children's picture books. If the *Noisy Books* offer young children entertainment in sensory experience and connections among literal environments, *The Important Book* shares suppositions with *The Little Island*, moving into philosophical and linguistic territories, questioning the very nature of objects as they are defined by different perspectives. The book opens with a title page that is preceded by the beginning of the text itself: "The important thing about glass is that you can see through it." An illustration of a glass, half-filled with water in which daisies stand, accompanies the text. In order to understand the text as well as the very nature of transparency, however, the illustration must define the narrative by contrast—the water and flowers are necessary in order to see the

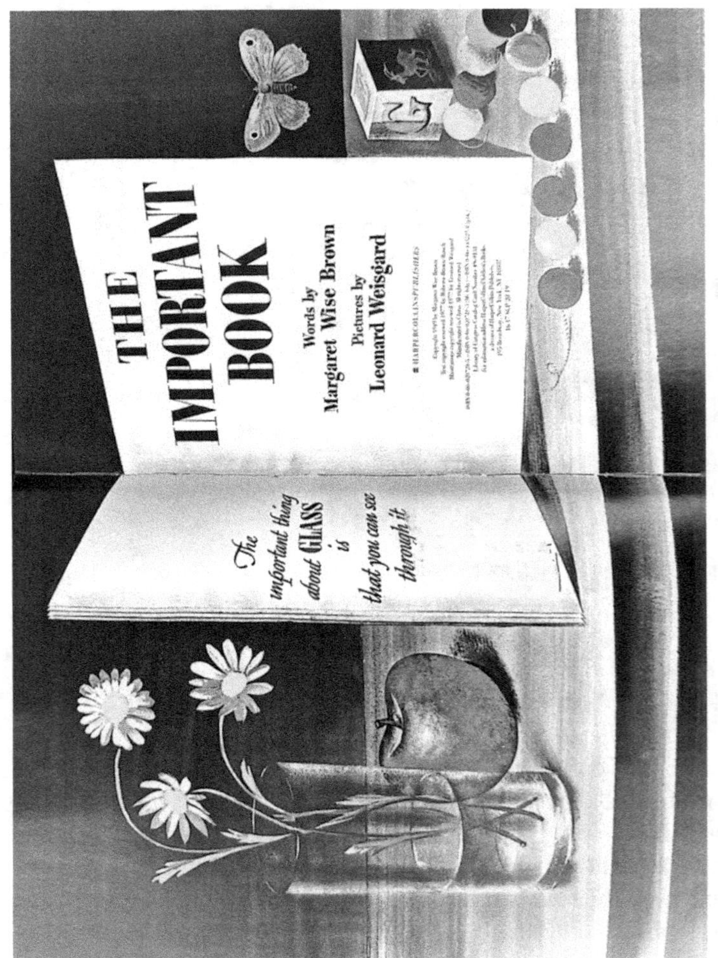

Figure 2.4 Brown, Margaret Wise. *The Important Book*. HarperCollins, 1949. pp. 1–2.

glass's transparency—in which case, the important thing about this glass is the presence inside of it.

Readers are immediately encouraged to begin questioning the book's textual statements as well as the ability to decide what makes an object distinctive at all. The following title page emphasizes this lesson as readers now must also dismiss their assumptions of traditional book structures.

The tendency to define by contrast appears in a number of other textual and illustrative relationships in this book. For example, Brown's narrative claims that "the important thing about a daisy is that it is white," and Weisgard's illustration shows that the whiteness of a daisy is only noticeable or even present when standing out against the other colors of blue, brown, and green in this picture. In fact, the white letters of the text are only visible because a dark brown tree trunk stands behind them. In another scene, raindrops stand on oak leaves, visible through a framed window pane, on whose glass lines of water show against the darker leaves behind. Here, "the important thing about rain is that it is wet," a tactile characteristic present in the drooping leaves and streaked glass. The contrast in these thought experiments encourages child readers to consider essence as defined by an object's impact on or against another object in the world, emphasizing materiality and relationship, as the Island and kitten do as well, discussed in *The Little Island.*

These ideas resonate with the developing ideas in the 1930s of the British school of object relations in which researchers argued that infants matured cognitively as they first defined themselves as part of the mother and later in contrast to the mother (Paccaud-Huguet 281). Brown and Weisgard here use their picture book to explore these relationships with which children might subconsciously relate. Human relationships to objects fill the pages of *The Important Book* as some objects are defined by their use: "The important thing about a spoon is that you eat with it [...] the important thing about a shoe is that you put your foot in it." The book's most studied page, the importance of an apple, states that an apple's essence is defined by its shape, "it is round," but the illustration here serves to take us back to the relationship between objects and people. This illustration, compared to René Magritte's famous "La chambre d'écoute" in an article by Anna Panszczyk, features one whole apple and one half apple sitting on a wooden table, above which hangs a window that looks out at a distant apple tree in a field. Although the text claims that roundness is the distinctive feature of the apple, the illustration represents each stage of the apple as it makes its way into the house to be consumed: the fallen apples on the ground around the tree contain the tree's seeds, its hope for new beginnings. The tree itself represents the growth of those seeds into maturation, and the fruit hanging from the tree's branches offers its usefulness to the table's owner. A ladder leaning against the tree's trunk represents the owner's gathering of ripe fruit, also shown in a full apple barrel standing beside the tree. Finally, the whole apple on the table shows the fruit's progression inside, finally resulting in its cutting and eating by the half apple in the foreground. The depiction of each of the apple's life stages proves its purpose in human consumption and its essential nature as defined by the presence of the human. Contrast and relationship are again prioritized in identification, just as the words and the pictures define each other.

Brown and Weisgard's book culminates, however, with the statement that "the important thing about you is that you are you." On this page, the book's object relations result in both a freeing and a constricting conclusion. The text appears to teach that our relationships with ourselves constitute the only contrast necessary to identify ourselves. Although objects may need an external presence to be understood, only the *youness* of "you," not your relationship with or contrast against others, defines an individual. This argument frees us to celebrate uniqueness and diversity, but it can also be limiting in an inability to reach beyond ourselves for communal identification. These competing tensions are heightened by Weisgard's use of Surrealism in his illustrations. While Brown's words encourage questions like "important to whom?" "who gets to chose?", Weisgard's pictures similarly conjure mystery: "the impulse behind the surrealist experience is to bring into question the concept of something we once thought to be firmly defined (like fur) and offer it a new association [...] the viewer is shocked into experiencing the strange" (Panszczyk 360). The alternating black and white and colorful illustrations as well as their sometimes surprising abstraction encourage readers to redefine these images for themselves, as well as the purpose of a picture book itself. Both Brown and Weisgard's *The Little Island* and *The Important Book*, then, extend their experimentation of author/illustrator collaboration to discuss questions of identity, perspective, and relationship.

A fairly sharp distinction from his experimental, Surreal, and Cubist images (including such titles with Brown as *The Poodle and the Sheep*

[1941], *Big Dog, Little Dog* [1943], *Red Light, Green Light* [1992], and *The Dark Wood of the Golden Birds* [1950]), Leonard Weisgard also found great success in his more commercial, elaborately decorated images. Even in this nostalgic style, however, Brown and Weisgard continued to create books that prioritize questions, experimentation, exploration, and discovery in stories such as *The Golden Egg Book* (1947) and *The Golden Bunny* (1953). In these texts, Weisgard created pages overflowing with color, natural life, ornate decoration, patterns, rounded lines, and texture. Weisgard's oldest child, Abigail, explained that Weisgard's "pictures are in praise of the abundance of the world and the sheer beauty of life" (qtd. in Marcus *Golden* 225). "Beauty" certainly describes this style aptly. The endpapers of *The Golden Egg Book* resemble those in *The Little Island*; both books open and close with collages of natural life, animals and plants layered upon each other in ways that suggest copiousness and plenitude. The difference in color, combined with the subsequent picture book pages, stylizes the two books differently, however. Whereas *The Little Island*'s endpapers present the natural world in black and white, followed by illustrations that emphasize line on calm pages, *The Golden Bunny*'s endpapers flash with color, followed by illustrations that emphasize soft ornamentation. Weisgard uses this inviting illustration to portray coziness, snugness, safety, and companionship.

The action in Brown and Weisgard's story all takes place in egg-shaped frames, outside of which the profusion of the natural world first established by the endpapers continues to explode. The first lines of text, "Once there was a little bunny. / He was all alone" suggest that the bunny's isolation is negative, but readers can see that the bunny is not alone; he is enclosed in the framing egg with another egg, in which "He could hear something moving inside." Although the story begins with a tragic character, Weisgard calms reader concern by assuring us that the bunny is still safe. Both the egg frame and the egg character within the story suggest safety in enclosed spaces, nurture, warmth, and all of these characteristics are associated with infancy in the egg, the young bunny, and eventually in the newborn duckling that emerges from the second egg. Brown and Weisgard here encourage curiosity within the safe confines of youth.

The bunny knows that something or someone must inhabit the egg, and as it considers the possibilities, the text and illustrations work together to create uncertainty, mystery, imagination, and suspense within safe boundaries. The two-page spread that portrays the egg's possibilities appears balanced, with two bunnies and two eggs on each page, both pages featuring the egg frame, and a short, grammatically parallel phrase associated with each possibility: "Maybe a little boy, / Maybe another bunny, / Maybe an elephant, / Maybe a mouse." The bunny begins to explore this mystery by experimenting with the egg, pushing it, jumping on it, throwing nuts at it, and even rolling it down a hill, "but still it didn't break. / And whatever was in the egg didn't come out." In Brown's story, the inhabitant of the egg gets to decide when it emerges; the outside world cannot impose its will on the egg to force out its occupant. In Weisgard's illustrations, many readers might be reminded that they inhabit an egg of childhood of their own, and they, hopefully, have agency to choose when to emerge from that safe enclosure. Although Brown and Weisgard would certainly have been aware of children forced from a protected childhood before they chose to leave it themselves, the artists offer child readers of all experiences a narrative here that allows time spent in the emotional safety and nurture of the book itself.

The picture book continues its contrasting representations of isolation and relationship with illustrations in which the egg and bunny appear together and those in which they are separated by text. They remain, though, enclosed in the egg-shaped frame and nestled down among the profuse flora and fauna that decorate the page outside of the narrative frames. Ken Chowder describes Weisgard's style as "decorat[ions of] the interior landscape of children's minds," pointing out yet another enclosure present for Brown's characters, the imagination of the reader. Although the bunny continues to explore the strange egg, this exploration poses no threat, anxiety, or pressure of anticipation in Brown and Weisgard's safe world, and the bunny remains relaxed enough to grow sleepy, to "beg[i]n to yawn. / And he yawned / and he yawned." He falls asleep, "curled up all sleepy and warm / close to the egg," which, of course, precipitates the duckling's hatching. The duckling provides a new inquisitor, a second character involved in exploration and discovery, and although the bunny is not enclosed in an egg, he is now safely enclosed in his sleep state, as safe as the duckling was in the egg. Brown questions the desirability of comfort and safety, however, when her text connects those conditions with isolation as the duckling says, "Inside the egg, / […] I thought I was all alone / in a small dark world." At this point, readers can see, safety may necessitate "small dark world[s]," and the risk of relationship exists in "a big bright world." Again, Brown and Weisgard emphasize the necessary conflict between individualism and relationship of *The Little Island* and *The Important Book.*

The Golden Egg Book becomes a near chiasmus in text and illustration as the duckling then repeats many of the bunny's original experiments. He pushes the bunny, jumps on him, throws a rock at him, and rolls him down a hill, actions all illustrated in the same two- to four-block page organizations of the bunny's earlier exploits. Each page remains framed by an egg shape, and most pages appear divided into two halves, paralleled by the opposite page. This blocking provides two-page spreads that usually include four groups of pictures, two on each side, during the scenes in which the animals experiment with the unknown presence.

The illustrations then tie the characters even more closely than a linear progression might. This theme is also cinched nicely on the last two pages of the book on which the bunny awakes, curious and inquisitive: "Where is my egg? / [...] And where did you come from?" The duckling redirects the bunny's priorities, though, answering, "Never mind that" / [...] Here I am." And this final line represents to readers that the answers to curiosity are only important, in the end, when they result in relationship and companionship, especially since "no one was

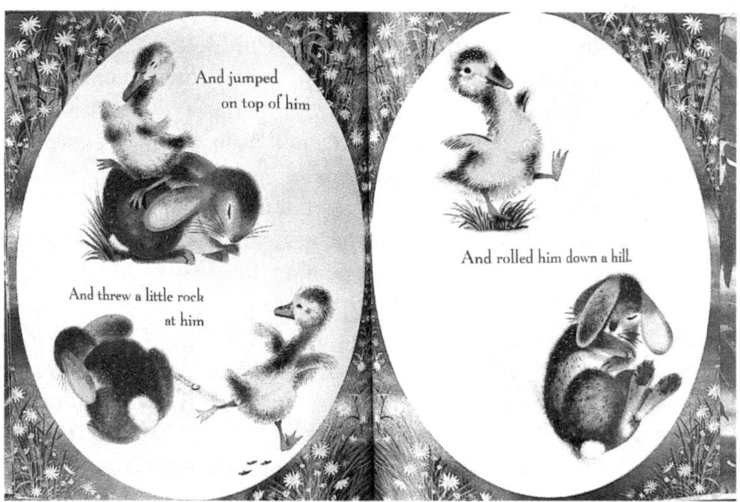

Figure 2.5 Brown, Margaret Wise. *The Golden Egg Book.* Little Golden Books, 1947. pp. 21–22.

ever / alone again." Once again, the collaboration between Brown and Weisgard, in the midst of their own creativity and exploration, leads to expression of connection and its importance, a theme for children that contrasted the usual Modernist theme of fragmentation.

These same ideas of companionship and isolation, individual identity and communal identity appear in other Brown and Weisgard collaborations, such as their 1947 *The Golden Egg Book* and their 1953 publication of the multi-genre *The Golden Bunny*. The two artists did not, necessarily, work through styles in any linear fashion; the combinations of Realism, Surrealism, and Traditionalism that all result in versions of Modernism intermittently appear in their publishing history. Instead, the friends seem to have been working through an exploration of these themes themselves and experimenting with different artistic styles in which to express their ideas. Regardless of the date, narrative, or artwork of these texts, Brown's work with Weisgard repeatedly returns to the importance of curiosity and exploration in search of identity formation.

Clement Hurd

Unlike Leonard Weisgard's prolific output for Brown's manuscripts, artist Clement Hurd collaborated with her on fewer projects. He knew Margaret Wise Brown, however, far more intimately than other artists' working relationships permitted. Clement Hurd and his wife, Edith Thacher Hurd, became important members of Brown's inner circle of friends and artists. As a well-to-do young man growing up under a successful banking father, Hurd graduated from Yale and expressed his desire to follow his own professional dreams as an artist. He traveled to Paris, where he worked under the classical painter Fernand Léger, returning to New York as a freelance artist. Unfortunately, the 1930s offered a difficult economic market for artists, and to make ends meet, Hurd took such jobs as painting murals on bathhouse ceilings. It was on one of these ceilings that Margaret Wise Brown saw Hurd's "Perils of the Sea" in Greenwich, Connecticut, which inspired her to meet the artist. Once acquainted, Brown introduced Hurd to William R. Scott, her future New York publisher of experimental children's picture books, and Hurd entered both Brown's professional life and her personal life as collaborator and close friend. Although Hurd illustrated over 100 picture books, many of which were projects between him and his wife as author, he continued to proclaim that "several artists," himself included, "produced their best illustrations for books by Brown" (Marcus *Dictionary* 57). Certainly, two of Brown and Hurd's collaborations remain canonical nursery books: *Goodnight Moon* (1947) and *The Runaway Bunny* (1942). In fact, the lasting popularity of *Goodnight Moon* appears not only in the 48 million copies that have sold since its 1947 publication, but also in such claims as scholar Robin Bernstein's pronouncement that "if you had to name one book to serve as the exemplar for all children's literature, Margaret Wise Brown's *Goodnight Moon* would be a plausible candidate" (877). *Goodnight Moon* and *The Runaway Bunny* earned Brown and Hurd international fame and lasting legacy, but Hurd also worked with such famous authors as Gertrude Stein. Although subsequent illustrators designed their own editions of Stein's picture book *The World Is Round* (1939), Hurd's initial interpretation "provided the only closely programmed not to say mimetic rendition of a Stein text" (Hubert 678). Hurd's sparse style is balanced in this text with depictions of animals that alter the animals' comparable sizes, but in retaining the balance, Hurd both encourages and tempers Stein's language games for children. Even this project, however, involved Brown as editor at Scott Publishing, the publishing house that some scholars credit with introducing "American modernist picturebooks" (Conrad 146). Hurd's foray into illustrating picture books began with his work on Brown's first publication, *Bumble Bugs and Elephants* (1938). This early collaboration and the life-long friendship it initiated established Hurd's reputation as one of Margaret Wise Brown's most important illustrators.

Hurd's incorporation of Modernist ideas into his picture book illustrations differs from Weisgard's primarily by more subtly incorporating Modernist ideology in lieu of explicit medium experimentation. Where much of Weisgard's work varies between styles and synesthetic expression, Hurd's illustrations remain much more mimetic, requiring a quieter Modernist strategy. On the title page of his very first picture book, for example, the word "Big" appears in larger type, and the word "Little" appears minimized. This theme continues throughout *Bumble Bugs and Elephants* (1938), with each picture representing the words exactly, rather than interpreting those words in a new way, as Weisgard might have done. In an article for *Modernism/*modernity, academics Renée Riese Hubert and Judd D. Hubert explain that "As had all image makers since the invention of the code and until Sonia Delaunay's and Blaise Cendrars' *La Prose* *du Transsibérien et de la petite Jehanne de France*, Hurd sought to enhance reading by providing plausible representations of some of the events and people described" (701). Although Hubert and Hubert apply this analysis to Hurd's illustration of Gertrude Stein's *The World Is Round* (1939), the technique is also famous in *Good Night Moon* as the pictures reflect each item to which the child bunny wishes a "good night." This more traditional picture book illustration strategy was not solely followed because of Hurd's intention; it was also largely prescribed by Brown herself. In fact, the image of the great green room originated in Margaret Wise Brown's mind as well as her reality, as her own bedroom included green paint, a red bedspread, a rocking chair, a table, and a black telephone (Gary 178). And, apparently, it took Hurd several revisions to capture those objects just the way Brown desired (Keyser). For some of her stories, Brown wanted, not realism exactly, but mimeticism that followed the lead her words established. In describing her work with Brown, Esphyr Slobodkina explained,

> Anytime I seemed to stray from the narrow path of strict honesty and complete integrity, [Margaret] raised loud, bitter objections. When I failed to draw the pics from nature and, instead, relied on some children's books [*sic*] illustrations, she returned the drawings with a cutting remark to the effect that why didn't I leave the cutie-cutie junk to Walt Disney and do my own, honest-to-goodness stuff.
>
> That remark was gratefully accepted and guided me [...] in all my subsequent work.
>
> (Qtd. in Marcus *Margaret* 229)

While the real representation of words by pictures could be stylized, in Brown's books, she often still required a respect for her child audience that resisted patronizing or infantilizing them.

Although much of Hurd's artistry for Brown emphasizes shape, line, and color over interpretive, experimental style, Clement Hurd created art that represented the Modernist movement as deeply as Leonard Weisgard's. His approach might best be understood in discussion with T.S. Eliot's famous 1919 essay, "Tradition and the Individual Talent." In this seminal thought experiment, Eliot emphasizes a balance between an artist's awareness and understanding of tradition—all the work of artists before—with individual talent—the contribution that a new, individualized perspective offers—in such a way that the entire tradition is slightly altered. Eliot points out,

> One of the facts that might come to light in this process is our tendency to insist, when we praise a poet, upon those aspects of his work in which he least resembles anyone else. In these aspects or parts of his work we pretend to find what is individual, what is the peculiar essence of the man. We dwell with satisfaction upon the poet's difference from his predecessors, especially his immediate predecessors; we endeavour to find something that can be isolated in order to be enjoyed. Whereas if we approach a poet without this prejudice we shall often find that not only the best, but the most individual parts of his work may be those in which the dead poets, his ancestors, assert their immortality most vigorously.
>
> (Eliot 54–55)

According to Eliot, the most original work can only be recognized in light of the tradition it joins. Then, reading this new contribution in its awareness of from whom it originates, our perception of the preceding texts slightly shifts. He explains, "what happens when a new work of art is created is something that happens simultaneously to all the works of art which preceded it" (55). New art changes old art because of the way the reader/viewer interprets the art, and its context will alter every time a new piece is added. In this way, the body of art is ever-growing, ever-aging, ever-transitioning as time passes.

In some ways, the picture book medium itself nicely represents Eliot's ideas. The combination of pictures and words both satisfies a reader's expectations of the genre while also requiring readers to learn how to decode the particular text of the present moment. Perry Nodelman explains,

> the pictures in a sequence act as schemata for each other. When a story is told in words as well as pictures, we first understand both the words and the pictures by means of the schemata we have already established for them – at first, our general expectations about stories and our general understanding about how pictures communicate. Then, the words correct and particularize our understanding of the pictures they accompany, and the pictures provide information that causes us to reinterpret and particularize the meanings of the words. Then all of that information becomes

> a schema for each new page of words and each new picture as we continue throughout the book.
>
> (Nodelman 217)

Just as new artistic contributions require an understanding of the established "schemata" or "tradition," according to Eliot, so might picture books, according to Nodelman. The new story and the "individual talent" that the story represents re-teaches the reader how to discern the meaning in each page as the narrative progresses. While Eliot recognizes this process as, ideally, occurring in all art, the picture book permits a heightened experience due to its combination of multiple art forms. Clement Hurd certainly employed Eliot's approach purposefully in his own art.

In *Bumble Bugs and Elephants*, Brown acknowledges "the pastness of the past" (Eliot 55) in the opening and closing lines of the text: "Once upon a time there was a great big bumble bug [...] Once upon a time there was a great big bumble bug..." (ellipsis in original). She situates her story within a fairy tale tradition, providing readers with a set of genre conventions to explain the narrative. We don't need to know what a bumble bug is exactly; it exists in the same world as fairies, dragons, and magic. In fact, the story ends where it began, as well, indicating that the tradition of the fairy tale continues after this book ends. *Bumble Bugs* is an addition, a contribution to this body of work, but it does also add something new, for while readers should be familiar with the butterfly, bird, turtle, and other animals of this story, the bumble bug is a new creation that can now be included in the fairy tale world. Hurd depicts this process visually. The first half of the book reveals the bumble bug, a dragonfly hummingbird hybrid, and five additional animals; readers then come to the center of the text, a scene in which three dogs occupy a dining room inside a home.

This double-page spread renders the only scene in the book that takes place inside, and this interior space is a domestic one. Although no humans appear on these two pages, they are strongly present in the prepared food on a decorated table, the décor of the tablecloth and two wall hangings, and the furniture itself, a table and chair, is clearly intended for human use, although currently occupied by the dogs. Very few people appear in *Bumble Bugs*, but their presence is integral, even central, to the narrative. Hurd uses this first half of the text as his own "tradition." He establishes visual themes of color, page design, shape, line, and character that readers then take as familiar into

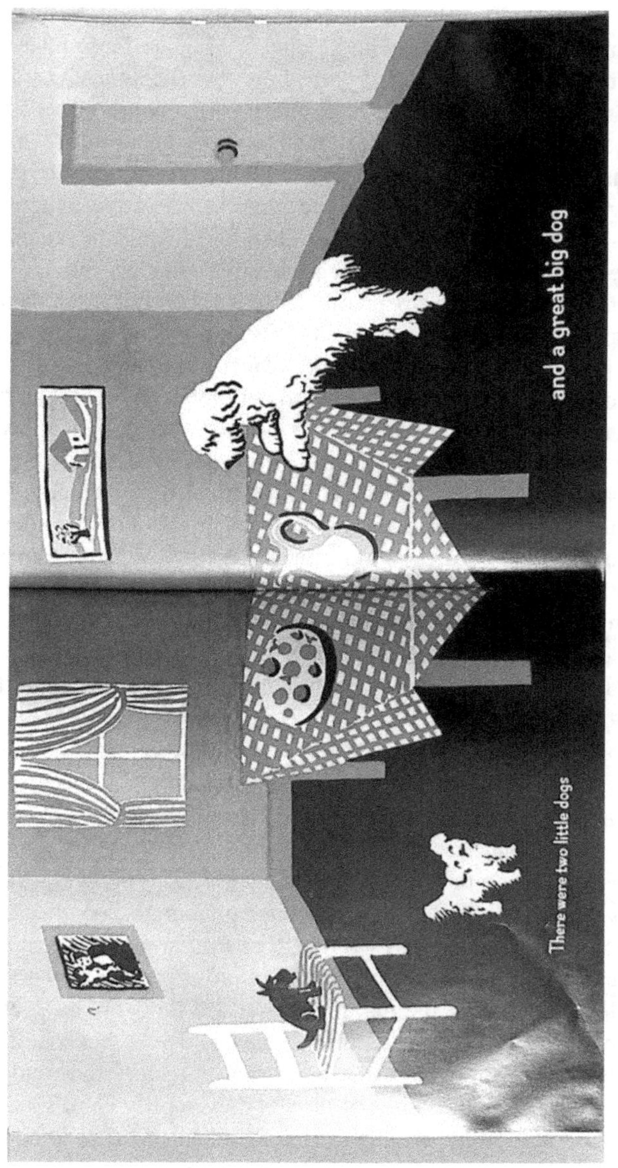

Figure 2.6 Brown, Margaret Wise. *Bumble Bugs and Elephants.* William R. Scott, 1938.

the second half of the book, which uses those expectations as building blocks to create something new.

The second half of Brown and Hurd's story continues to introduce new characters, pigs, horses, and elephants, but on those pages also appear characters from the first half of the text. These cameos do not begin until the book's second half. On the pigs' pages also pop in a rooster and a butterfly; the horses have to share their spread with five chickens and two turtles, and the elephants are accompanied by a bird, a butterfly, four chickens, and three pigs. Whereas the first half of *Bumble Bugs* constitutes a tradition, a "handing down," the second half uses the "simple currents" already established and adds "novelty" in a way that may encourage a reader to be "most acutely conscious of his place in time, of his contemporaneity" (Eliot 55). The final two pages of this picture book, then, invite the reader, now aware of both the tradition and its place in the present, to contribute an individual talent by asking in black letters across white pages, "What do you know that is great big? What do you know that is tiny little?" At this point, the child reader may become an artist, Eliot's "poet," who "must develop or procure the consciousness of the past and [...] continue to develop this consciousness throughout his career" (55). In the microcosm of the first picture book Hurd collaborated on with Brown, he simply mimicked in illustration the words on each page and yet demonstrated one of the dominating artistic philosophies of the Modernist era.

Hurd extended this expression of temporal awareness and artistic contribution even more clearly through his work on *Goodnight Moon* and its sequels. Published in 1947, *Goodnight Moon* demonstrates its enactment of Eliot's "handing down" by depicting on the first two-page spread of the "great green room" two references to Brown and Hurd's previous publication of *The Runaway Bunny* and the nursery rhymes from which their literature emanates (55). Following *Bumble Bugs and Elephants*, Brown and Hurd collaborated on the second most popular text of Brown's career, *The Runaway Bunny*, in 1942. This story appears twice in *Goodnight Moon*'s great green room, first as an illustration from the narrative hangs on the wall and, second, as the book itself, open to its title page, lies on the bookshelf. The references to this previous work, appearing in picture form only and never mentioned by the words of the story, exemplify Hurd's gestures to his own tradition in such a way that stimulates readers to consider how *Goodnight Moon* now "modifies" Brown and Hurd's "existing monuments," "ideal order," and the way it is now "altered" (Eliot 55).

For, although readers may have understood *The Runaway Bunny* as a story of a mother promising to pursue relationship with her child no matter the child's future path in life, now that another bunny child, maybe slightly older, appears in *Goodnight Moon*, the references to the first story in the second story can inspire new questions about *The Runaway Bunny*. For instance, is this the same child bunny? If so, is the female adult in *Goodnight Moon* his mother or grandmother, as the illustrations appear to depict an older figure with her knitting and rocking chair? If it is not his mother, then where has his mother gone, and why is his grandmother now the one putting him to bed? As children's literature researcher Daniel Pereira notices, "What happens in *Goodnight Moon*, however, is that the parents have vanished, recalling the old lady to take their place" (169). Is this "old lady" babysitting, or have the child bunny's parents passed away, in which case *The Runaway Bunny* would take on a whole new meaning? Certainly, the intertextuality of *The Runaway Bunny*'s appearances in *Goodnight Moon* may alter the interpretative tradition that Brown and Hurd had created in their previous work.

Secondly, *Goodnight Moon*'s great green room also integrates allusions to nursery rhymes, namely "The Cow That Jumped Over the Moon" and "The Three Little Bears." Both of these allusions appear as wall hangings depicting scenes from stories that remain part of a tradition of bedtime storytelling and that mimic Brown's own childhood bedroom. As a girl, Brown had shared a room with her sister, Roberta, in Beechhurst, Long Island, and their room featured a fireplace framed with decorative ceramic tiles. These tiles "depict[ed] nursery rhyme characters—the Three Little Bears and the Cow That Jumped Over the Moon that Margaret would recall in *Goodnight Moon*" (Marcus *Margaret* 12). Hurd's incorporation of these allusions, at Brown's request, therefore, serves to establish Eliot's "tradition" in two ways. First, they point to the literary tradition of nursery rhymes into which *Goodnight Moon* now steps as a new bedtime story. Second, they evoke a nostalgia for Brown's own past childhood as well as the parent reader's childhood, a nostalgia reawakened and reinforced by the presence of a new "individual talent" in the bunny child and human child reader. These bedtime scenes have occurred before and will occur again as the heritage of struggle between the parent and child at bedtime continues through generations.[2]

Clement Hurd's reliance on such Modernist ideas as T.S. Eliot's continued on an even larger scale following the publication of

Goodnight Moon. With the success of this immediately canonical children's nursery book and its establishment as "one of the most universal cultural references," Hurd and Brown used *Goodnight Moon* as its own traditional cosmos from which to publish new talent (Keyser). Goodnight Moon could be considered its own "existing order" or "historical sense" due to its monumental influence as it spawned numerous progeny, first by Brown and Hurd, then by Hurd alone, and finally by other authors (Eliot 55). In fact, the same year that Harper published *Goodnight Moon*, Harper & Row also put out *Goodnight Moon ABC: An Alphabet Book* (1947) that advertises itself on the cover as "based on the book by Margaret Wise Brown." In this sequel, intertextuality is central, again using references to *The Runaway Bunny* and nursery rhymes but relying primarily on *Goodnight Moon* for its illustrations, which have been cut directly from the original text and enlarged to represent each letter of the alphabet. This second book is only possible because of its predecessor; the words and pictures would have no meaning without their referents in *Goodnight Moon*.

Two years later, Brown and Hurd publish another book in their *Goodnight Moon* series, *My World* (1949), "a companion to *Goodnight Moon*." This third installment, again, relies on the "tradition" of *Goodnight Moon* and offers an "individual" story that extends outside of the green room into other parts of the bunny child's physical world. The text includes illustrations that incorporate pictures from *Goodnight Moon* with minimal alteration and add new context, such as the fireplace or the lamp, curtains, chairs, and even the wall painting from *The Runaway Bunny*. These illustrations, more than the words of the narrative, take readers back to the "pastness" of *Goodnight Moon* and then highlight what has been added. And just as *Goodnight Moon* motivates a re-reading of *The Runaway Bunny*, so too does *My World* encourage reassessment of what readers thought they understood about *Goodnight Moon*. In this new story, for instance, it appears that the "old lady" of *Goodnight Moon* is, indeed, the child bunny's mother, not grandmother, as the same character reappears, and the text refers to her as "Mother." *My World* also introduces a father, or "Daddy," who parents and even replaces the mother figure in a fishing scene, reminiscent of *The Runaway Bunny* plot. *My World* definitively expands the narrative tradition started by *The Runaway Bunny* and continued by *Goodnight Moon*.

Following Brown's death in 1952, Hurd published one additional accompaniment to the series in 1984, a pop-up book titled *Goodnight*

Moon Room. After Hurd's own passing in 1988 of Alzheimer's, Harper published the *Goodnight Moon* wall calendar in 2002, *Goodnight Moon 123: A Counting Book* in 2007, and *100 First Words* in 2020, all listed as written by Margaret Wise Brown and illustrated by Clement Hurd, even decades past their deaths. These subsequent publications continue to capitalize on the work done by Brown and Hurd and fail to contribute any new "talent" that Eliot encouraged in Modernist artists. This move that occurred in the *Goodnight Moon* series following *My World* marked a shift away from artistic contributions created for children and into marketing schemes targeted at consumerism. Rather than a "poet" working on these texts and using a mind or "a receptacle for seizing and storing up numberless feelings, phrases, images, which remain there until all the particles which can unite to form a new compound are present together," the later *Goodnight Moon* installments are simple reprintings of earlier art recombined in new ways without adding anything new (Eliot 72). In this process, they lose their spark and individuality, failing to contribute much to the tradition at large. More successful that these later books "by" Brown and Hurd are picture books by other artists, playing on the tradition established by *Goodnight Moon*. Peggy Rathmann's *Good Night, Gorilla* (1994) has successfully relied on Brown and Hurd's structure and won such awards as *Parenting Magazine*'s Best Children's Book of 1994 and earned designations such as an ALA Notable Children's book (1994).[3] Artists like Rathmann continue to offer new talent that relies on an awareness of and contribution to a literary tradition of which Eliot, Brown, and Hurd most likely would have been proud.

Incorporation of Modernist theories such as Eliot's is not the only demonstration of Hurd's experimental drive, however. His use of color, or lack thereof, also reveals Hurd as a Modernist. In 1919, the Académie Julian in Paris was teaching Chevreul's Law of Simultaneous Contrast of Colors: "This contrastive use of a limited colour palette combined with abstracted, minimal shapes and large swaths of white positive-negative space [...] [creates] a tempered modernist look" (Conrad 139–40). This Law appeared in many Modernist picture books, including Macmillan's Happy Hour Book series and in Clement Hurd's own illustrations for Margaret Wise Brown. *The Runaway Bunny* and *Goodnight Moon* are excellent examples of Hurd's use of this technique. Professor Joseph Stanton explains the black and white pages of *The Runaway Bunny* as illustrating "some of the basic details of each episode" while the colored pages "represent the heart of the action" (9). In the black and white drawings, the mother and child bunnies appear on separate pages in separate scenes, except for the opening page which depicts the child bunny running from his mother. The colored two-page spreads, however, depict the bunnies in a single scene, usually still separated on different pages, but connected by the color and location of the action. It isn't until the last two colored drawings that the mother and child appear together. The use or absence of color thereby indicates relationship or isolation, respectively, through the adoption of modern visual art techniques.

The presence and absence of color in *Goodnight Moon* works similarly, again depicting wholeness and community or individuality. While the great green room repeatedly appears in full-color illustrations, when the child bunny wishes a good night to each object separately, those objects appear only in black and white. Wholeness, completeness, and unity appear in color while distinctiveness or difference appears in black and white. Hurd stated that "Without doubt, my pictures for *The Runaway Bunny* (1942) and *Goodnight Moon* are considered my best work" (qtd. in "Hurd" 393). He continued to use color in careful ways, however, in other texts. In his 1955 publication with Brown, *The Little Brass Band*, rather than alternate between color and black and white, all of Hurd's illustrations appear in color, but the color palette remains small, using only yellow, green, orange, black, and white. Similarly, in *The Peppermint Family* (1950), Hurd paints in red, blue, black, and white, and these limited palettes cause objects to be depicted in unusual colors, such as his bright yellow skies in *Little Brass Band*. For such a mimetic illustrator, the experimentation often surfaced in color use rather than object depiction.

Leonard Weisgard may have drawn from a wide variety of artistic styles, playfully synthesizing sound and image, moving between Surrealism, Realism, and ornate representation, but his work with Margaret Wise Brown often returned to themes of understanding the self in relation to the outside world as well as emphasizing safe curiosity and exploration. Clement Hurd, on the other hand, created a single artistic world in his work for Brown. Most of his images are immediately recognizable as his. The theme that he and Brown most often explored through these images, in contrast to Weisgard's individuality, was interconnectedness with the child at the center.

This theme has already surfaced in discussion of *Bumble Bugs and Elephants*; the structure of the book's plot is circular, both beginning and ending with "once upon a time," and the central pages of the book depict an interior, domestic space. The animals build and join each other as the story progresses, and although humans are rarely visually present, they remain central in many of the animals' purposes—for example, the horses are introduced as cart horses, doing work for people. *Goodnight Moon* also works in circularity, connecting each of the objects in the bunny's room with the child reader surrogate. Although the story runs linearly, from bedtime to sleep, that line progresses in overlapping circles, starting with the whole room, moving to focus on a couple of objects separately, and then moving back to the wholeness of the room again. The plot focuses on the way that the objects connect to the bunny; he may be the center of his own universe, "the child in the midst of his world of things," but he is the center of that interconnected world (Stanton 13). These attachments create a sense of coziness, safety, familiarity with a focus on "comforting interior space" (Stanton 11).

Brown and Hurd's 1947 publication of *Goodnight Moon ABC*, so shortly after publication of *Goodnight Moon* itself, provides a nice example of this thematic emphasis. Of course, the intertextuality discussed above, both its status as a sequel and the allusions to *The Runaway Bunny* and nursery rhymes, naturally connects the text to other narratives. This alphabet book also works as a seek-and-find experience, as the back cover instructs: "From kittens to stars to yarn, there are so many things that can be found in the great green room. Search for them all as you learn your ABCs." The purpose of this text is to recognize the way that individual elements connect with each other to form wholes. The story opens with two double-page spreads that list individual objects, air, the clock, the fireplace, the dollhouse, each representing a letter of the alphabet. The third double-page spread shows the entire great green room, in which readers can look for the objects just named individually.

Readers need to return to these pages to continue looking for the objects listed through the rest of the book, as they all have their context, their significance, only because of their contributions to the wholeness of the room. Even when the outside is depicted, on the letter "O" page, it is framed and contained by the curtain and windowpanes, for even exterior spaces are relevant only because of their relationship to the interior's security. In addition, Brown and Hurd create layers of coziness and connectedness that amplify kinship feelings. Representation of the dollhouse, for example, depends on layers of interiority. The "house," standing for the letter "H," provides an inner space within

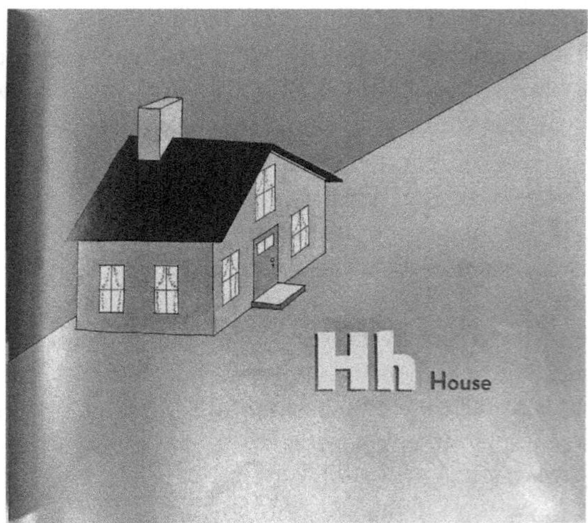

Figure 2.7 Brown, Margaret Wise. *Goodnight Moon ABC: An Alphabet Book*. Harper & Row, 1947. p. 4.

the nucleus of the bunny's room, which exists within the bunny's larger house. This page shows a house within a room within a house, firmly positioning the reader in a connected, womb-like, heart space. Similarly, the "I" page reminds readers that the narrative takes place "In the great green room," and the "U" page specifically situates the child bunny "Under the covers." The layered positioning of objects, protagonist, and readers foregrounds themes of comfort, safety, and connection.

The Little Brass Band provides another example of a Brown/Hurd collaboration with a similar theme, outside of the *Goodnight Moon* universe. This narrative tells the story of a band of brass players and their instruments, collecting one morning near a Renaissance-era village, playing music as they move into the town where they perform a concert. Afterwards, they play as they depart and one by one drop out of the song as they reach their homes. It is music, in this book, that represents the individuality of the players, individuality that works best and creates community when played together. Each instrument comes from a different place—the trumpet "from a distant farm," the drum "in the valley," the bassoon at "the crossroads," and two "golden horns" from the top of a hill, while "a flute, a clarinet, and an oboe were waiting on the bridge." Each instrument is pictured separately, and most have their own pages. Once they join each other, however, "on the bridge," the band is pictured together, even bridging page gutters in their companionship. Once this band reaches the town, they continue to create connection, first among both "the old people" who listen from windows and "the children" who dance in the streets. Then the "littlest house in town" is also joined to "the biggest house in town" both by the music and the coins that the townspeople shower upon the band members. Finally, the narrative's climax occurs as the band links the whole town at their concert in the town square where all different types of listeners come to enjoy the music. Following this crescendo of interrelationship, the band departs, dropping players off at their homes, "farther and farther and farther" until "nothing but the lonely sound of the trumpet" is left, ending as the player enters his house and closes the door. This band's music connects, and the individuality of each instrument, "lonely" by itself, contributes to celebration, to community, when joined by others. Although each has something to offer in solitude, it is the joy of connection that Brown and Hurd valorize in this text.

Leonard Marcus postulates that "Margaret turned primarily to [Hurd] to illustrate those manuscripts of hers that investigated the child's elemental feelings of attachment to home" (*Margaret* 93). This interpretation certainly appears correct, although "home" is depicted in different ways through their collaborations. Home can be a place, even a place within a literal house, but it can also be in community, in connection, in tradition, finding a way to contribute to the whole's good.

Garth Williams

Unlike Weisgard and Hurd, Garth Williams was not discovered by Margaret Wise Brown but was, instead, introduced to her by her editor at Harper, Ursula Nordstrom. In fact, authors Elizabeth K. Wallace and James D. Wallace suggest that Nordstrom was so pleased with William's illustration success of *Stuart Little* in 1945 that she sought to continue his career with her by pairing him with the prolific Brown, who she knew would have plenty of texts to illustrate. This plan worked nicely, as he eventually collaborated on ten books with Brown, amidst achieving independent fame with his drawings for Laura Ingalls Wilder's *Little House on the Prairie* series (1932–1943) and E.B. White's *Charlotte's Web* (1952). Williams's more mainstream popularity combined an artistic ability to capture movement in black and white with emphasis on line and to choose "exactly the right detail or set of details from a myriad of possibilities" that could indicate a much broader sense of place or situation (Wallace 71). For children's stories specifically, Williams's talent lie in capturing the "sensations and images of infancy, childhood, and youth" in a way that satisfies the nostalgia that many adult readers crave and many child readers enjoy (Scott Elledge qtd. in Wallace 106). For this reason, certain of Williams's illustrations have achieved canonical status, defining the narratives just as strongly as their words. Images of Laura's covered wagon, the grass of the open prairie, and the family's little house of felled logs captures and then can later raise again the adventures of Laura, her family, and the mystery of American settlement in viewers' minds. Williams's images of Fern nursing Wilbur and the Arable children swinging in Uncle Zuckerman's barn evoke associations of maternal care and childish playfulness. And the detail of Williams's depictions of hair, fur, grass, and softness perfectly partner Brown's themes of coziness, safety, and home. Beyond the reflections of children and their experiences, though, Williams is most often remembered for his animals:

> As a survey of his major drawings from this period reveals, Williams' most significant contribution to children's literature lay in the unique fashion in which he was able to create animals. Though they possess human traits, and often engage in human activities, these animals remain unmistakably animalistic.
>
> Avoiding the trap of projecting the human onto the animal at the expense of the beast, Williams created creatures who remind us of our affinity to the natural world.
>
> (Wallace 122–3)

Certainly, the temptation of children's book illustrators to draw animals that look like children may remain strong, but most of Brown's collaborators avoided that infantilization of their subjects. Indeed, both Weisgard and Hurd produced animals that appeared even less anthropomorphized than Williams's, but it is Williams's animals that find an ideal balance that makes them so memorable. Rather than anatomically precise depictions of creatures, as Weisgard skillfully produced for *The Little Island*, or abstract suggestions of animals, as

Hurd created in *Bumble Bugs and Elephants*, Williams creates such characters as dogs, bunnies, and owls that appear both realistic and relatable. Indeed, Barbara Badar argued that Garth Williams "shared with Margaret Wise Brown [...] a softness and warmth free of sentimental haze" (257). It was precisely the childishness of his characters without any of the denigration that the term can often connote that elevated Williams to such estimation.

Garth Williams's introduction to Margaret Wise Brown by Ursula Nordstrom does not suggest lack of relationship between the illustrator and author. In fact, Brown grew quite close to Garth and his wife, Edith, working and relaxing with them as both professionals and friends. The close relationship lasted until Brown's untimely death in 1952 and proved itself meaningful in their presence at many of her life's celebrations. The story behind Garth Williams's illustration of *Wait Till the Moon Is Full* (1948) belies his emotional support of Brown, as Wallace and Wallace relate it. Although Clement Hurd initially illustrated Brown's story of a young raccoon whose mother repeatedly urges him to "wait till the moon is full" to leave their burrow at night, it is Garth Williams's illustrations that ultimately saw publication. Hurd, himself, claims that his depiction of the story "was the finest single piece of work he had ever done," but due to Hurd's hesitation to support Brown's relationship with Michael Strange, Brown chose Williams as illustrator, a friend she knew fully encouraged her tumultuous romance (Wallace 135). The author and illustrator's kinship seems to have resulted in skillful work as they enjoyed "the closest and happiest kind of collaboration, swapping ideas, criticizing each other's efforts, and provoking each other's best work" (Wallace 4). While Leonard Weisgard illustrated the largest number of Brown's texts and Clement Hurd illustrated her most famous books, Garth Williams, arguably, enjoyed the closest relationship to Brown as well as achieved some of the greatest notoriety in an individual career among those illustrators who worked on Margaret Wise Brown books.

Like Weisgard and Hurd, in addition to other contemporary artists, Garth Williams practiced Modernist art in his production of children's literature, primarily in his Surrealist tendencies, but also through his participation in Modernism's enjoyment of nostalgia. For these reasons, "it is certainly possible to claim—based on an unusually large body of extraordinary art, one that is widely recognized for its precise and telling use of detail sometimes verging on the surreal; its ironic whimsy conveying emotion without sentimentality—that Garth

Williams was one of the most important illustrators of the twentieth century" (Wallace 4). His successful incorporation of the surreal is most quickly noted in his work for Brown's *Little Fur Family* (1946) and *Mister Dog* (1952). As a response to Golden Books' publication of *Pat the Bunny* in 1940, Harper & Brothers published *Little Fur Family* six years later, including a fur jacket to encourage the kind of tactile interaction that *Pat* had introduced. Beyond inviting readers to complete different kinesthetic tasks, as *Pat the Bunny* does, *Little Fur Family* moves into characteristically complex Margaret Wise Brown territory in exploring identity themes. Brown and Williams's story introduces a fur child who spends his day journeying out from his home to explore the world around him, then returning for dinner and a cozy bedtime at night. The defining feature of this family is its fur, particularly since the characters' animal identities are unclear, ranging from possible bear to cat to dog. It is their defining feature that they layer upon themselves by donning "little fur coats," fur slippers, boots, and hats. While the layering of fur parallels Brown's narrative layers of coziness and safety, both physically and relationally in this story, it also carries a sharper edge of discomfort, of shock, commonly produced by Surrealism, as readers consider where the fur the characters wear came from. Since people don't wear clothing made from human skin, Brown and Williams's story takes a concept readers would feel comfortable understanding, that is wearing fur, and considers it in the light of Surrealism by putting that same fur on fur creatures. Suddenly, a natural choice feels unnatural at the exact same time that it increases the snugness of the text.

The story progresses after the father ventures for the day "into his little fur world," and the fur child endures his mother's domestic chores of bathing and dressing him. The child then practices a masculine trajectory by leaving the home and playing in the "wild wild wood," a wood illustrated as dark and potentially threatening with muted colors. Here, the fur child temporarily loses his clothing, which goes unexplained in the text, and his sneezing indicates an allergy to the wild: "Other uncanny and dreamlike effects in William's illustrations add to the surreal atmosphere of *Little Fur Family*" in addition to the fur family's fur clothing (Wallace p. 130).[4] Specifically, this atmosphere feels most heightened when the fur child comes across a "little tiny tiny fur animal" that looks just like himself. Amid his adventures in the wood, the little fur child has three encounters with other creatures. These three encounters comprise an episode distinct from the rest

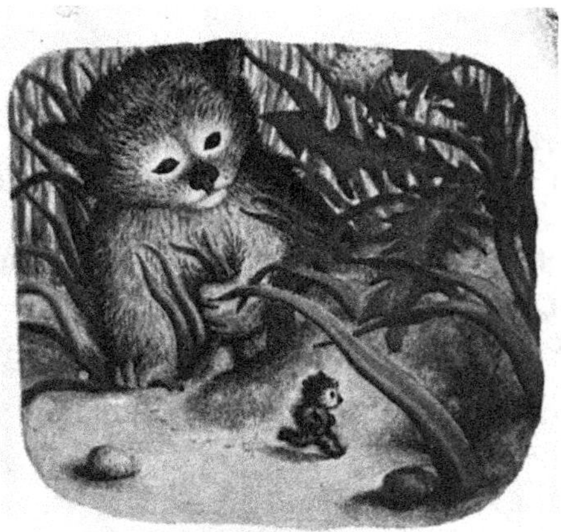

Figure 2.8 Brown, Margaret Wise. *Little Fur Family*. HarperCollins, 1946. pp. 17–18.

of the story, as the child suddenly and without explanation appears without his clothes, and the illustrations noticeably brighten in color and light. First, the fur child "came to a little river full of fish." The fur child watches these Other creatures, whom he differentiates from himself by noting that, "The fish didn't have any fur." He then pulls a fish out of the river, out of its natural environment, to inspect it, then throws it back after, as Williams's illustration shows, he stares at it face to face.

Second, the fur child reaches "into the air," a second foreign environment for him, and catches a flying bug, illustrated as a ladybug, which also "didn't have any fur." After looking at this second Other, he again throws it back, having finished using it to understand himself better. Third, though, the fur child catches a tiny fur animal, shown running in grasses. Rather than throwing it, however, the fur child kisses it "right on its little fur nose" and replaces it "gently back in the grass." This kiss symbolizes his acceptance of the miniature version of himself, a reflection of which he approves. The moment includes Surrealism due to the strangeness of the fur child, unidentified as any one recognizable animal readers may know, finding another creature just like himself, but smaller. His apparent love for the creature resolves the uncanny moment though, and the story returns to themes of safety and affirmation in his return home on the next page. This central episode with the fur child's encounters with the fish, the insect, and the tiny fur animal, comprise his exploration in the big world, resolved by returning home, fully dressed. Within the tale of domesticity and coziness lies a Modernist, surreal exploration of self that involves rejection of the Other.

Mister Dog (1952) also demonstrates the Modernist Surrealism employed in Brown and Williams's collaborations while representing Williams's skill at anthropomorphizing animals without compromising their natural origins. Mister Dog, named Crispin's Crispian and modeled on Brown's own beloved pet, not only lives alone and "belongs to himself," but also adopts a child that he invites to live with him, subverting the expected relationship between animal and human child. Crispin's Crispian models an adult character as he wakes himself, feeds himself, walks himself, and even buys a bone for his own dinner, which he explains as getting "his poor dog a bone," even though he is that very dog, speaking of himself in third person. This strange relationship with himself, both owner and owned, both first and third person, constitutes the story's purpose. Crispin's Crispian has achieved a dual identity by both living in a disempowered space, as his dog-ness demands, and claiming power of ownership over himself, through acting the role of the adult domestic. This duality allows Crispin's Crispian to live within the confines of his natural state while also subverting those confines. The applicability of Mister Dog's surreal situation is explicitly interrogated when he finds a little boy. The little boy immediately asks Crispin's Crispian, "Who are you and who do you belong to?" When Crispin's Crispian answers this question and then asks who and "what" the little boy is, he receives the answer that the boy also belongs to himself. Rather than the story of a child coming across a stray animal and adopting it, in Brown's story, the dog adopts the stray child as he invites, "Come and live with me." Not only may the child reader see herself in Crispin's Crispian's character, as a disempowered character who can still take responsibility for herself, but she can now also recognize herself in the child character, Crispin's Crispian's partner in self-ownership. The rest of the story progresses in parallelism both in text and picture as it follows the two in their daily tasks, each embodying a disempowered state but then claiming ownership of that state, resulting in a happy ending of balanced companionship free of power differentials.

Although Brown and Williams did not as overtly demonstrate Surrealism as did Brown and Leonard Weisgard, moments in their stories certainly expose the movement's influence on their art. And even beyond Surrealism, Brown and Williams expressed their Modernist experiments, maybe somewhat surprisingly, through incorporation of nostalgic themes in some of their stories. Wallace and Wallace explain that Williams's "illustrations often conjure a vanished agrarian lifestyle, tapping into a powerful postwar yearning to connect with a distinctly American past" (5). While much of Modernist focus celebrated the new and the experimental, it also less famously included a looking back to pre-World War cultures before industrialization and mechanization increased feelings of isolation and loss. The limbo between the past and present created much of the unrest that Modernism strives to capture in its art (Rasula 2). This awareness of time and change again appears clearly in *Little Fur Family*, specifically in the juxtaposition between domestic space and wild space.

There is a marked anxiety in this text which appears immediately on the book's opening endpapers as an illustration of the little fur child standing alone with an unhappy look on his face and his hand, worriedly, at his mouth. The second illustration alleviates the tension, showing the whole family together, the parents watching the child play. This opening dichotomy establishes a disapproval of solitude and a joy in familial companionship, a dichotomy established in the pictures only. The story itself then begins with a painting of the home space—the fur family's cozy tree. Here, children's literature scholars Perry Nodelman and Mavis Reimer's home-away-home plot structure begins in the home, continues through the fur child's explorations in the "wild wood" and concludes with his return to his family. The two spaces are illustrated very differently, communicating contrasting messages that resolve in nostalgia. For instance, the fur family's home is illustrated using bright, saturated colors, where the characters are clothed, fed, and bathed. The space indicates safety and comfort in contrast to the wood which appears in darker, muted tones, even when the text describes it as "dark and sunny." As the child naturally explores the wilder world into which his father ventures and his grandfather lives, and returns home safely, the tone of the illustrations as well as such pictures as the opening portrait of the little fur child still indicate a valorization of home and family life over maturation, growth, and independence. In fact, the return to the home includes physical reconnection with the parental characters as the fur child "bumps" into his mother, who takes him into her arms. His father than carries his child on his back up to bed where the story ends with the

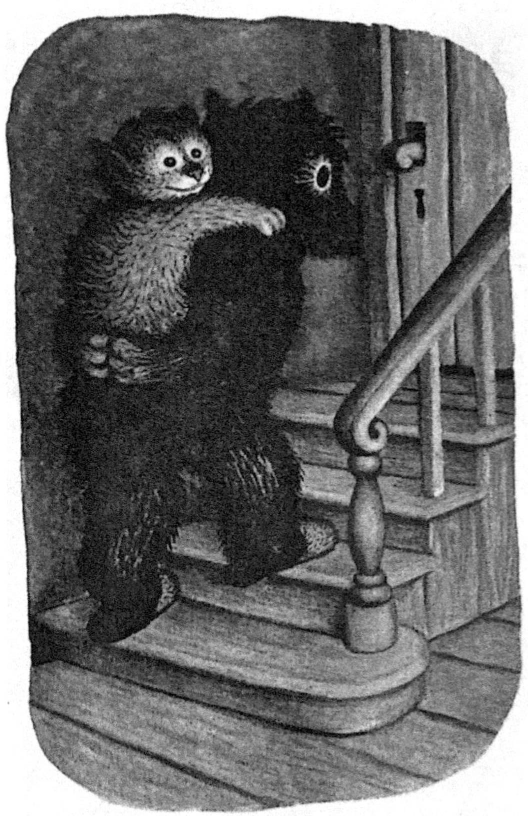

Figure 2.9 Brown, Margaret Wise. *Little Fur Family*. HarperCollins, 1946. pp. 23–24.

father, mother, and child all physically linked in a beatific illustration of comfort.

Finally, the closing endpapers repeat the initial representation of the solitary fur child, again pictured in his anxious state. The fur child may have a very successful day in exploring his world and progressing in identity differentiation, but the illustrations add a secondary story that prioritize the nuclear family in the domestic space over the independent child in the wild world.

This Modernist ambivalence over progression appears in Brown and Williams's *Wait Till the Moon Is Full* (1948) as well. In this story, the child raccoon eagerly anticipates leaving the safe domesticity of his burrow home, but his mother continues to encourage him to "wait" until the end of the month. Although the great drive of the story resides in the child's progress toward maturity, the illustrations again indicate a contrast of desires. The opening endpapers in this story show the raccoon mother moving toward her tree burrow, lighted against the dark twilight in which she walks.

The bare tree branches show a strong wind, against which the mother clasps her thin shawl and a watching owl uses his open wings to balance. The mother's expression is serious, even melancholy, and her home draws every line of her body toward its security. Once the story begins, Williams's illustrations offer warm sienna as the only color amid black and white line drawings. This simplicity implies a cleanliness, a comfort, a softness in their lack of intensity, and this environment allows the raccoon child safely to imagine the world above. Even in these colors, however, the words used to describe the bigger world include "wind," "black branches," "big silence," and "dark." With the rising of the full moon, however, these more foreboding terms change to depict the night scene as one of fantasy and play. Again, where some sections of the story encourage a threatening perspective of the wider world, adjacent pages show it to be mysterious and captivating.

Most of the story comprises the mother and son's conversations about the outside world, and each character's depiction demonstrates a different directed tension to express their separate desires, to stay and to go, respectively. The mother repeatedly faces left, into the burrow, away from the entrance and what lies outside. Her body positions reinforce her efforts to keep her son inside, safe, and infantilized. The child, however, often faces and moves right, toward the door and natural progression forward. Similarly to *Little Fur Family*, this child protagonist also has a small version of himself in the form of a baby raccoon toy. At times, even when the raccoon child faces left, his toy peeks out behind him, facing right and representing his deep desire to leave the home, even as he presently obeys his mother's wishes. Unlike *Fur Family*, the child's longing to go outside lies in his yearning for community as he vocalizes that he wants to "find another little raccoon to play with." The mother's nostalgic drive inward and backward clashes with her son's pull as she appears to believe that

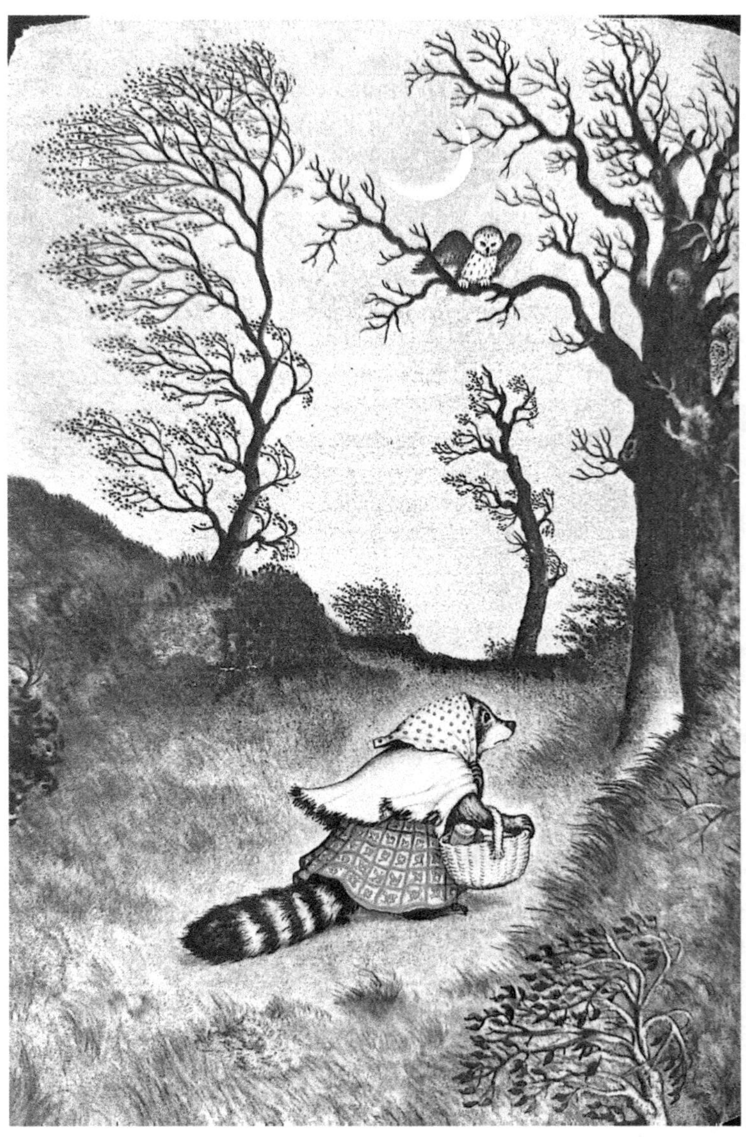

Figure 2.10 Brown, Margaret Wise. *Wait Till the Moon Is Full*. HarperCollins, 1948. p. 1.

external community is best experienced at a particular time, a quintessential Modernist clash. When the full moon returns and the time for the child raccoon to leave the nest arrives, the illustration again bursts into full color, representing the completeness and vibrancy of life in relationship. Unlike *Fur Family*, the plot structure does not resolve back at home but, instead, demonstrates progress in maturation as the time for change and growth has permanently changed the child raccoon's life. Regardless, both texts share a sense of nostalgia in the safety of the domestic space that the children leave to develop their identities.

It is these very themes of identity, the individual and the community, and a sense of belonging that Brown particularly covered in her works with Williams. Although Brown and Weisgard explored the connections between individuality and community, as in *The Little Island*, and Brown and Hurd explored the magnetism of the home, as in *Goodnight Moon*, Williams's books with Brown often included a sense of belonging. In their work on *Home for a Bunny* (1956), for example, the artists address this individuality and community. The bunny protagonist recognizes that his needs in a type of home differ from the robin and the frog. Even the groundhog, living under a tree as a bunny could do, does not want the companionship of the bunny. These animals are individuals with different needs. Community is still cherished, however, as the book teaches, through the protagonist's discovery of another bunny who does welcome the traveler into her home. Like *The Golden Egg Book* or *The Little Brass Band*, this story values both solitary character and community relationship. Brown and Williams extend this theme in *Home for a Bunny*, however, by imbuing the story with a sense of belonging that goes further than simply discovering companionship. *The Golden Egg Book* offers its characters friendship, but *Home for a Bunny* offers its characters a home, a place of affinity that may or may not include someone else. Illustrator William Joyce explains that he finds Garth Williams's worlds especially appealing because "His characters all looked like they were very pleased and comfortable with who they are. They had such presence. And all their little habitats looked like the nicest, coziest, safest places you could ever find" (qtd. in Marcus *Golden* 136). Williams's characters belong in their spaces. This is also an important theme in *The Sailor Dog*, published in 1953. A big part of Scuppers's appeal is how neat and organized he keeps his boat, his recognition that even his hat, his rope, his pants, his spyglass, his shoes, and his own body have appropriate spaces in the little room below deck. Scuppers is an independent, adventurous spirit who realizes that "here he is where he wants to be—a sailor sailing the deep green sea." Scuppers explores individuality and community, but his identity is finally predicated on belonging at sea where he can be most himself.

Margaret Wise Brown never specifically stated that she chose work for different illustrators based on particular themes she wanted to convey. In fact, there were times when she allowed multiple artists to illustrate the same story and then decided which set of illustrations she liked best. In studying the collaborations, however, there certainly appear strains of ideas or development of thoughts that Brown continued with individual artists. Many of her texts explore identity as well as the very American ambivalence in balancing individuality with communal relationship, but certain illustrators then seemed to bring out refinements of these themes in their own ways. Wallace and Wallace note that "Illustration is the bastard child of the fine arts: often the offspring of rigorous artistic training and sheer inspiration, it is rarely perceived as a 'legitimate' and freestanding creative art [...] Especially when an artist draws for someone else, he is seen merely to express, to supplement, or to serve the author's words" (2). In looking at the collaborations between Brown and her illustrators, though, we can clearly see her disapproval of such perspective. Each of Brown's illustrators brought important work to her texts in discrete ways as well as contributed to Modern art for children. Brown did not collect picture book illustrators; she collected artists, and their production, both individually and communally, enhanced the value of children's literature.

Notes

1 In needing to choose from Brown's extensive list of collaborators for constraints of space, I choose the three illustrators with whom she published the largest number of texts. They appear in decreasing order of volume.

2 As Robin Bernstein notes in her article on the going-to-bed-book tradition, "The ritual of an adult reading out loud to a child at bedtime formed mainly in the second half of the nineteenth century and achieved prominence in the early twentieth century in tandem with the rising belief that soothing rituals were necessary for children at the end of the day" (878). These literal traditions are both noted and built upon in *Goodnight Moon* in the form of Hurd's illustrations of the process and within the process.

3 This genre of bedtime book has grown large and includes titles such as David Cunliffe's *Good Night Little Turtle* (2014), Mark Jasper's *Good Night Dinosaur* (2013), and Adam Gamble's *Good Night Our World* series (2006–2018).

4 Some of the story elements in *The Little Fur Family* harken back to Beatrix Potter's *Peter Rabbit* (1901), including the style of the painted illustrations with cameo-like, fuzzy edges, the child protagonist's loss of clothing, the resolution with the child tucked into bed, and even Peter Rabbit himself sneezing as he hides from Mr. McGregor in the watering can. But unlike the didacticism of *Peter Rabbit*, the little fur child does not disobey his parents, and his exploration of the bigger world is encouraged, as it results in a safe return home, with the wisdom of his place in the world.

References

Badar, Barbara. *American Picture Books from Noah's Ark to the Beast Within.* Macmillan, 1976.

Bernstein, Robin. "'You Do It!': Going-to-Bed Books and the Scripts of Children's Literature." *PMLA*, 135, 5, 2020, pp. 877–94.

Brown, Margaret Wise. *Big Dog, Little Dog*, illustrated by Leonard Weisgard. Doubleday, Doran & Company, 1943.

———. *Bumble Bugs and Elephants*, illustrated by Clement Hurd. William R. Scott, 1938.

———. *Goodnight Moon*, illustrated by Clement Hurd. Harper, 1947.

———. *Goodnight Moon ABC: An Alphabet Book*, illustrated by Clement Hurd. Harper & Row, 1947.

———. *Home for a Bunny*, illustrated by Garth Williams. Golden Books, 1956.

———. *Mister Dog: The Dog Who Belonged to Himself*, illustrated by Garth Williams. Little Golden Books, 1952.

———. *My World*, illustrated by Clement Hurd. Harper, 1949.

———. *Red Light, Green Light*, illustrated by Leonard Weisgard. Scholastic, 1992.

———. *The Dark Wood of the Golden Birds*, illustrated by Leonard Weisgard. Harper, 1950.

———. *The Golden Bunny*, illustrated by Leonard Weisgard. Simon & Schuster, 1953.

———. *The Golden Egg Book*, illustrated by Leonard Weisgard. Little Golden Books, 1947.

———. *The Important Book*, illustrated by Leonard Weisgard. Harper, 1949.

———. *The Little Brass Band*, illustrated by Clement Hurd. Harper, 1955.

———. *The Little Fur Family*, illustrated by Garth Williams. Harper 1946.

———. *The Little Island*, illustrated by Leonard Weisgard. Doubleday, 1946.

———. *The Peppermint Family*, illustrated by Clement Hurd. Harper, 1950.

———. *The Poodle and the Sheep*, illustrated by Leonard Weisgard. Dutton, 1941.

———. *The Runaway Bunny*, illustrated by Clement Hurd. Harper, 1942.

———. *The Sailor Dog*, illustrated by Garth Williams. Little Golden Books, 1953.

———. *The Seashore Noisy Book*, illustrated by Leonard Weisgard. Harper, 1941.

———. *The Summer Noisy Book*, illustrated by Leonard Weisgard. Harper, 1951.

———. *Wait Till the Moon Is Full*, illustrated by Garth Williams. Harper, 1948.

Chowder, Ken. "There was no one like Leonard." *Leonard Weisgard: Author and Illustrator of Children's Books*. 1 May 2018, http://leonardweisgard.com/leonard-weisgard/.

Conrad, JoAnn. "Modernity and Modernism in Twentieth-Century American Picturebooks." *International Research in Children's Literature*, 12, 2, December 2019, pp. 127–53.

Eliot, T.S. "Tradition and the Individual Talent." *The Egoist*, September 1919, pp. 54–55, 72–73.

Gary, Amy. *In the Great Green Room: The Brilliant and Bold Life of Margaret Wise Brown*. Flatiron, 2016.

Hubert, Renée Riese & Judd, D. Hubert. "Reading Gertrude Stein in the Light of the Book Artists." *Modernism/*modernity, 10, 4, 2003, pp. 677–704.

Hurd, Clement. "Shayne Rayburn." *Continuum Encyclopedia of Children's Literature*, Letter H, pp. 393–4.

Keyser, Hannah. "11 Fascinating Facts About *Goodnight Moon*." Mentalfloss, October 19, 2020, www.mentalfloss.com/article/64005/11-fascinating-facts-about-goodnight- moon.

Marcus, Leonard S. "Back to the Future." *The Horn Book Magazine*, 86, 1, 2010, pp. 38–41.

———. *Golden Legacy: The Story of Golden Books*. Golden Books, 2007.

———. *Margaret Wise Brown: Awakened by the Moon*. Beacon, 1992.

———. "Margaret Wise Brown." *Dictionary of Literary Biography: American Writers for Children, 1900–1960*, edited by John Cech, vol. 22. Bruccoli Clark, 1983, pp. 42–70.

———. "Seen and Heard: Margaret Wise Brown and Leonard Weisgard's *The Noisy Book*." *Story Time: Essays on American Children's Literature from the Betsy Beinecke Shirley Collection*. Yale UP, 2016, pp. 191–203.

———. "Shape Shifter: Leonard Weisgard's Quest for the Modern in American Picture Book Art." *The Art of Leonard Weisgard*. The Eric Carle Museum of Picture Book Art, 8 March–8 June 2016.

Mitchell, Lucy Sprague. "Margaret Wise Brown, 1910–1952." *Children Here and Now: Notes from 69 Bank Street*, 1, 1, 1953, pp. 18–20.

Nodelman, Perry. *Words About Pictures: The Narrative Art of Children's Picture Books*. University of Georgia Press, 1988.

Paccaud-Huguet, Josiane. "Psychoanalysis after Freud." *Literary Theory and Criticism*, edited by Patricia Waugh. Oxford UP, 2006, pp. 280–97.

Panszczyk, Anna. "This Is Not about Picture Books: From 'Here and Now' to Surrealism in Margaret Wise Brown's Little Fur Family and The Important Book." *Children's Literature Association Quarterly*, 36, 4, 2004, pp. 359–80.

Pereira, Daniel. "Bedtime Books, the Bedtime Story Ritual, and *Goodnight Moon*." *Children's Literature Association Quarterly*, 44, 2, Summer 2019, pp. 156–72.

Rahn, Suzanne. "Cat-Quest: A Symbolic Animal in Margaret Wise Brown." *Children's Literature*, 22, 1994, pp. 149–61.

Rasula, Jed. *History of a Shiver: The Sublime Impudence of Modernism*. Oxford UP, 2016.

Rathmann, Peggy. *Good Night, Gorilla*. G.P. Putnam's Sons, 1994.

Salisbury, Martin. *100 Great Children's Picture Books*. Laurence King, 2015.

Stanton, Joseph. "Goodnight Nobody: Comfort and the Vast Dark in the Poems of Margaret Wise Brown and her Collaborators." *The Important Book: Children's Picture Books as Art and Literature*. Scarecrow, 2005, pp. 7–17.

Stein, Gertrude. *Writings 1932–1946*, edited by Catherine R. Stimpson & Harriet Chessman. The Library of America, 1998.

Wallace, Elizabeth K. & James D. Wallace. *Garth Williams: American Illustrator, A Life*. Beaufort Books, 2016.

Weisgard, Leonard. "Caldecott Acceptance Speech – July 2, 1947." *Leonard Weisgard: Author and Illustrator of Children's Books*, http://leonardweisgard.com/caldecott-acceptance-speech-july-2-1947/.

3 The Philosophic Artist

Margaret Wise Brown's books respect their child readers, demonstrated in the quality of their writing and the high art they offer in the artistic collaborations with visual artists. Thematically, they address mature ambivalences in identity and community engagement as artifacts of Modernism. But, perhaps most audacious for these board books and nursery fodder are Brown's philosophic undercurrents. Her narratives achieve fuller depth and richness when read in light of their advanced theoretical concerns. Until the past few decades, literary critics often used philosophical studies to contextualize children's literature and to comment on its dual audience, while philosophers sometimes used children's literature to exemplify philosophical theories. It remains a more contemporary argument, however, to recognize children's literature as purposefully philosophically informed and effective. Aristotle (384–322 BCE), for example, argued that children and young people were incapable of philosophy or politics, a conception continued through René Descartes (1596–1650), Christian Wolff (1679–1754), and even Anthony Krupp, whose 2009 publication *Reason's Children: Childhood in Early Modern Philosophy* limits children's abilities to think philosophically (Costello xiii). In such twentieth-century philosophical thought led by Peter Costello, Matthew Lipman, Gareth Matthews, Karin Murris, and Tom Wartenberg, however, children's "philosophical lives" emerge alongside the

> need to engage them on their own terms, by listening to and facilitating the peculiar way that they come to acts and texts, in order to allow them to say what is real, who they are, and what ought to happen.
>
> (Costello xiv)

DOI: 10.4324/9781032727028-4

The act of engaging children "on their own terms" certainly appears throughout their literature, as authors and scholars of children's literature have recognized in their wide use of cultural, historical, existential, psychoanalytic, and phenomenological movements to write and to read this literature. What these adults, alongside contemporary philosophers, acknowledge is the capabilities of children to theorize their worlds, even if the adults in their lives often failed to recognize it. Margaret Wise Brown stands as an important example of a children's author who addressed children on more sophisticated philosophical levels than was common in the mid-1900s, an address led by Brown's interest in Modernism art movement. Such literary influences as Gertrude Stein and Virginia Woolf encouraged Brown, influencers whose own writing was deeply informed by different philosophies. Brown has become identified along with these Modern authors "for whom the multiplicity of selves—rather than the fostering of a single, balanced, possessed self—was of utmost importance and delight" (Estes 169). Leonard Marcus, in his biography of Brown, points to the child bunny in *The Runaway Bunny* as an example of one of Brown's characters who physically represents the continual change that a child encounters in his "expanding sense of self" (*Margaret* 156).[1] Such representations reveal Brown's fearlessness in addressing abstract, subjective experience as an experience that her own child readers live. For instance, Brown's exploration of self-individuation, Object Relations, and relationships to time demonstrate her interest in reflecting back to child readers their own subjective experiences.

Commonly understood as sharing the same root questions, inquires in psychology and philosophy often overlap. Stemming from classical considerations of the human experience and scientific research into physiology, psychology moved into explorations of the human mind and the impact of external experience on internal processing in the nineteenth century. The psychology field grew, quickly dividing into branches of study such as cognitive, developmental, and social psychologies. Some branches found homes more naturally among academics and others among scientists, but educators and pediatricians discovered a particular interest in the development of the human brain, resulting in developmental psychology and early childhood development theories. Margaret Mahler (1897–1985) arrived on this scene in the 1950s to define the separation-individuation process and to extend Object Relations theories first surfacing in the 1920s and 1930s. A successful Hungarian pediatrician, Mahler had studied at the classical Vienna Psychoanalytic Institute, building a foundation in a "structural theory of mind with the ego as one of its primary subjects" (Wolfs 3). These Freudian ideas contributed to her definition of the separation-individuation process, a process during which a child develops an individual sense of self as separate from the primary caregiver. This "key contribution to the field of developmental psychoanalysis" includes the necessary childhood differentiation between self and external objects before recognition of personhood (Wolfs 1). This recognition of physical individuality can then grow to mental and emotional individuality over time. These ideas, as well as more traditionally philosophical theories of time and its subjective experience in childhood, surface in Margaret Wise Brown's writing. Brown's own increasing awareness of such inquiries informs certain of her narratives as she represents childhood experience.

One example of a Brown text that engages in complex, philosophical relationships that young children must regularly navigate is the 1949 self-proclaimed companion to *Goodnight Moon* (1947), *My World*. In concert with the same illustrator as *Goodnight Moon*, Clement Hurd, *My World* follows the visual style of its predecessor closely in illustration, alternating color and black and white pages, and depicting the same bunny family characters. Readers of *Goodnight Moon* will also recognize identical furniture pieces, like the mother's/grandmother's rocking chair and the fireplace, as well as the intertextual reference to Brown's *The Runaway Bunny* in an illustration from that text on the wall in the family's dining room (the illustration also appears in the child bunny's room in *Goodnight Moon*, as discussed previously). One central difference between the two stories, however, is the child bunny's age. Although indeterminate, his age in *Goodnight Moon* is most likely older than his age in *My World* because, in *My World*, he still sleeps in a crib. In *Goodnight Moon*, the child bunny has graduated to an adult bed. This difference makes *My World* a prequel to *Goodnight Moon*, and it accordingly addresses psychological and philosophical issues relevant to a younger child. Published second, however, this story spatially opens the world introduced in *Goodnight Moon* to a larger house, even acknowledging the distant city and the modes of transportation available for departing the domestic sphere. Where *Goodnight Moon* remains limited to the child bunny's bedroom and, briefly, the night outside the window, *My World* addresses a larger spatial life. *Goodnight Moon* investigates the more mature, psychological fears of dream states and the unconscious, while *My*

World, on the other hand, remains interested in earlier psychological stages, practicing and/or rapprochement, defined by Margaret Mahler as parts of the separation-individuation process, in identifying objects, space, and time in the contained "world" of the child bunny's home. Therefore, Brown and Hurd provide the less developed characters room to learn and grow while creating a more confined yet safe and more intimate space for advanced experiences.

The separation-individuation process, according to Mahler and her colleagues, includes

> the establishment of the sense of separateness from, and relation to, a world of reality, particularly with regard to the experiences to *one's own body* and to the principal representative to the world as the infant experiences it, the *primary love object.*
>
> (Mahler et al. 3, italics in original)

In other words, it is the process during which an infant begins to recognize the self psychologically as an individual, separate and distinct from a parent, usually her mother. The necessity of this process proceeds from what Mahler called "symbiosis," or oneness assumed by the infant with the caregiver. Mahler's research argues for this process as usually beginning between the fourth or fifth months of life and continuing through the thirtieth to thirty-sixth months, constituting the separation-individuation phase. This theory developed in tandem with Object Relations theory, a theory largely constructed by Sigmund Freud but descending in research from such philosophers as Aristotle. Freud's work, as early as 1905, addressed the ego's pathological development and the development of object relationships, providing a foundation for Mahler's research. Mahler's colleague Fred Pine explains,

> As Freud had studied the object as that thing (person, body part, inanimate object) through which drives are gratified, [Mahler, Pine, and Bergman] would go on to study how the infant's ego first constructs a notion of the object (now the whole, other person), differentiates itself from that object, and forms an attachment to it.
>
> (viii)

Mahler's book outlining the separation-individuation process, *The Psychological Birth of the Human Infant: Symbiosis and*

Individuation, did not appear until 1975, but both Freud's ideas and Mahler's own research, papers, and lectures appeared much earlier. Therefore, although Margaret Wise Brown's *My World* was published twenty-six years before Mahler popularized the term "separation-individuation," these ideas were circulating and developing among Freud's and his successors' research as Brown wrote her children's books. It should not be surprising, therefore, that Brown depicts the separation-individuation process as it is impacted by other Modern philosophical definitions and conceptions of objects and the world.

As the picture book opens, *My World*'s child bunny first identifies himself by possession and exploration of objects around him. This exploration performs Aristotle's object inquiry. In Aristotle's *Physics* II 3 and *Metaphysics* V 2, the philosopher describes the four "causes" he sees necessary to understand if we want to know an object: the efficient cause, which describes the motivation for its creation; the formal cause, which describes its appearance; the material cause, which describes what it is made of; and the final cause, which describes its function or purpose (Falcon 2). Margaret Wise Brown's bunny child explores the formal and final causes of objects he finds in his house and then identifies himself through ownership. For instance, the child bunny considers, "Mother's chair. / My chair. / A low chair. / A high chair. / But certainly my chair." In exploring these pieces of furniture, the bunny child differentiates their physical appearances, "low" and "high," but ultimately finds greatest applicability to himself by his possession of the "low" chair. In this way, he processes a psychological moment using a philosophical inquiry of reality.

This process continues through the picture book in a stream-of-conscious manner, and the bunny child often substitutes consideration of an object's formal cause with a brief narrative of final cause, both stating knowledge of the final cause and extending analysis of it: "My dog. / Daddy's dog. / Daddy's dog / Once caught a frog." Here, the relation to the object once again begins with consideration of possession, but then skips formal cause to process narratively an aspect of the dog's final cause: dogs catch things. The bunny child returns to consideration of formal cause in regard to his toy Bear when he states, "Daddy's boy. / Mother's boy. / My boy is just a toy / Bear." The first few lines end with full stops, suggesting that these are truths the child has firmly decided upon. He then recognizes the formal cause of his own "boy"; it looks like a toy, but then his final line demonstrates that he still engages with that object as more than just a toy with capitalization of "Bear." The child bunny may know that his bear is a toy, but it emotionally remains another Presence in his life.

Demonstration of his familiarity with objects' causes also reveals the bunny child's desired control over his world. In a bathroom scene, he narrates, "My soap. / Daddy's soap. / My soap will make soap-suds, I hope." Once again, the child recognizes possession, states final cause, then uncovers an insecurity that his object will not perform its final cause the way his father's does. Will it still be soap if it doesn't sud? Will he still be himself if the soap that belongs to him does not act the way that his father's soap acts? These questions address a common childhood anxiety of control and performance in the child's hope to mimic an adult. Some of the objects he considers are shared objects, specifically the dog and the cat pets who belong to the family at large. When the pets enact their final causes, however, they are attributed to the adult's possession. At other times, objects are named and possessed, with no other cause mentioned. These pages, "My toothbrush. / Daddy's toothbrush. / My comb. / Mother's comb," keep the priority of identification focused on possession more than on any other attribute. For Margaret Wise Brown's child protagonist, the psychological process of separating from his parents and creating an individual identity includes sustained thinking about the presence, function, and ownership of objects.

The spatial placement of the bunny characters and their objects in *My World* represents a second source of identification for the bunny child as part of his individual, subjective experience of life. Immanuel Kant describes space as a subjective experience:

> Space is not something objective and real, nor a substance, nor an accident, nor a relation; instead, it is subjective and ideal, and originates from the mind's nature in accord with a stable law as a scheme, as it were, for coordinating everything sensed externally.
>
> (qtd. in Janiak 1 par. 1)

In his illustrations for Brown's text in *My World*, Clement Hurd visually represents the idea of subjective space by placing figures and objects in psychologically meaningful spaces. For example, the book's opening page shows two copies of *My World*, the very book the viewer is reading, overlapping each other and identical except for size. The text explains that one copy belongs to the bunny child and the

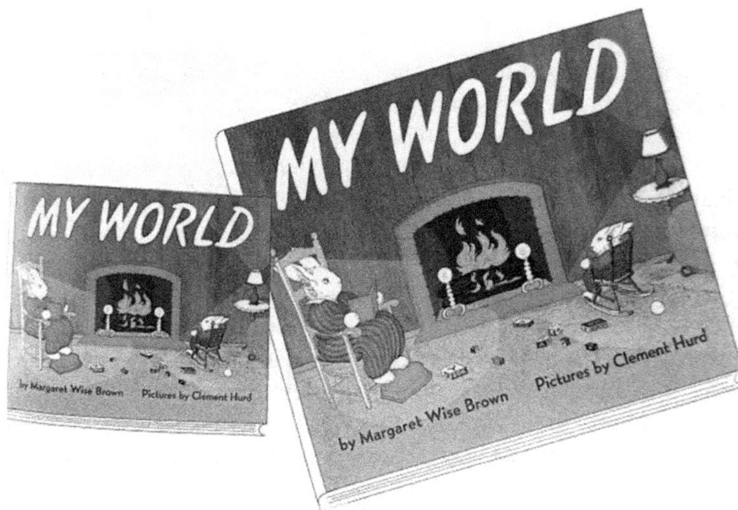

My book. Mother's book.
In my book I only look

Figure 3.1 Brown, Margaret Wise. *My World.* HarperCollins, 1949. p. 1.

other belongs to his mother; the books represent the two characters, and they do so while touching, joined, connected.

This initial illustration depicts the bunny child's subjective perspective of space as it represents his "symbiotic" connection to his parent (Mahler et al. 3). As *My World* continues, however, this perspective changes. The very next page moves viewers into the book cover itself, removing the book edges' framing device and placing us within the scene depicted on *My World*'s cover—the same cover reproduced twice on the opening page. Now, viewers are inside the bunny child's world, and inside, the characters occupy their own spaces. The mother bunny appears on the left-hand page, and the child bunny appears on the right, separated both by the fireplace and the physical book's spine. The characters remain connected by facing each other and even looking at each other, rather than at the book or the fire the text describes, but a separation has begun on this page. Similarly, the balance between individual identity and familial connectedness continues onto the following page where the characters disappear, but their objects remain to represent them. The left-hand page shows the mother's chair, occupied by the child's toy bear next to the child's slippers. The right-hand page shows the child's chair, occupied by a pair of pajamas (whose pajamas remains unclear as the text lists both the child's and the father's pajamas) next to the father's slippers. Although the central objects carrying the most visual weight, the chairs, are separated by the book spine again, they face each other in the companionship of objects belonging to other family members. These illustrations represent the child bunny's developing separation-individuation through subjective space.

As the story continues, illustrations begin depicting the child bunny and his parent on opposite pages, facing away from each other. Examples include a page where the father and his son work on their cars in matching mechanics' suits. Engaged in identical activities in identical outfits, the characters still occupy their own spaces, physically and mentally. The later bathroom scene shows the father bunny and child bunny involved in different hygienic activities, brushing hair and brushing teeth, respectively, on their own pages, in different clothes, facing away from each other. Although connected by the space of the bathroom, the two characters continue to move farther apart psychologically.

Pages continue with additional examples, but there are exceptions as well. In two full-color scenes without text, Brown's and Hurd's bunnies appear together as a single-family unit. In one illustration, the father bunny checks his watch as he stands over his son, asleep in a crib. In another, the family eats around the dinner table with a visiting bunny family, each family contained within its immediate unit but divided between families by the book spine. These two pages as well as others provide assurance that, as the bunny child continues to separate from his parents, he does so by choice, and those parents remain attentive, involved, and watchful. Even with clear spatial distinctions between family members, as the child matures, psychological connections remain, represented by subjective space.

Time constitutes a third source of identification for Brown and Hurd's protagonist in *My World*. Philosophers have developed multiple overlapping theories of time and how we experience temporality, but these diverse theories can generally be grouped into three central distinctions, named by philosopher Barry Dainton: the Cinematic Model, the Retentional Model, and the Extensional Model of time. Briefly, the Cinematic Model constitutes early experiences of time in which awareness is limited to the frame of the moment. Thinking beyond the present in any direction has not yet developed. The Retentional Model remains based on present experience but includes recognition of change within those presents. Seeing and understanding that change allows awareness of the recent past as well. Finally, the Extensional Model describes the ability to extend recognition of time into the past or future, to step beyond present experience (Dainton 1.1.1 pars. 5–7). Due to cognitive growth, the models often parallel physical and mental maturity so that childhood growth might be mapped to the evolution of the conscious awareness of time. The differences between awareness of time in *My World* and *Goodnight Moon* reflect this evolution.

Goodnight Moon depicts a single bedtime routine, and time passing is represented by the light in the bunny child's room fading from a brighter light to a darker room as well as two clocks that mark time passing on subsequent pages. There is a clear, linear progression shown in *Goodnight Moon.* In *My World,* however, the younger bunny child does not process time as a linear sequence of events; instead, his days are more episodic and stream-of-consciousness. The differences between these perceptions of time exist because the older child bunny in *Goodnight Moon* has matured philosophically to understand the Retentional Model of time in which an individual is capable of perceiving a present moment as well as remembering a limited, temporary past (Dainton 1.1.1 par. 6). Brown's older child can remember a past long enough to consciously experience a more linear timeline as the sun sets, the moon rises, and the child falls asleep. The younger child in *My World,* however, remains limited to a Cinematic Model of time:

> our immediate awareness lacks any (or any significant) temporal extension, and the same applies to the contents of which we are directly aware – they are akin to static, motion-free 'snapshots' or 'stills'. Our streams of consciousness are composed of continuous successions of these momentary states of consciousness. In this respect they are analogous to movies, which (as displayed) consist of rapid sequences of still images.
>
> (Dainton 1.1.1 par. 5)

My World's child bunny processes time as a series of snapshots to which there is no apparent order or explanation. Some scenes take place at night, others in the morning, and still others as possible dreamscapes.

The time of day for the child bunny appears delineated by activity. The child bunny narrator explains, "I go to sleep / When my story is read, / When my prayers are said, / And when my head / Is sleepy on the pillow." He does not recognize a bedtime according to clock time or even the sun's placement. Instead, time remains dependent on his actions. Similarly, breakfast means morning: "My breakfast. / My morning. / Daddy's breakfast. / Good morning." Again, time revolves around the child rather than around nature or a timepiece. This conception of time differs from his parents' who, of course, use clocks to structure their days. The illustration that depicts the father bunny putting his son to bed includes a watch in the father's hand, which he checks as he stands over his son's crib. This mechanical time indicates the father's ability to anticipate and interest in future time: What time did his son fall asleep? What does that time indicate about the time he will wake? How much time is left before the father must head to bed himself? This Extensional Model of time includes the ability to recognize a "succession of these extended 'chunks' of experience" (Dainton 1.1.1 par. 7). Likewise, the text-less page showing the bunny family at breakfast includes a clock on the wall. Although the bunny child explains that, for him, morning means eating breakfast, his parents prepare for the day using a mechanical timepiece. The three models of experiencing time depicted in *Goodnight Moon* and *My World* further represent the separation-individuation process of the child bunny. The younger bunny in *My World* defines his day, his world, and himself according to his activities. As he ages, in *Goodnight Moon*, he grows able to understand time in a more compressed, linear fashion, the continued development of which is modeled by the bunny parents and the house clocks. This one text encompasses an array of philosophical inquiries that the bunny child makes about his world, inquiries into objects, space, and time that help him in the psychological process of separation-individuation.

The many pages of analysis Brown permits her bunny child to explore his reality philosophically are supported by inclusion of a particular classic English folktale. Margaret Wise Brown's concern with the child's perception of self in relation to the world further appears in *My World*'s allusions to "Goldilocks and the Three Bears." Fairy tale scholars Iona and Peter Opie report that the 1837, fourth volume of *The Doctor* by Robert Southey included the first print version of

"Goldilocks" (260). Although the narrative has changed much since, and probably before then, the central thrust of this folktale involves a story of identification and the situation of self in reality. Childhood studies critic Oliver Rose argues, "Fairy tales live as long as they are in accord with some deeply rooted perception of reality" (86). In the case of Goldilocks, the character tests a number of familial options in order to decide for herself which role fits most comfortably; Goldilocks individuates from parental figures. In response to psychoanalyst Bruno Bettelheim's claim that the story makes no Freudian sense, Rose retorts, "Goldilocks tests both Mother and Father, and finds both not evil, but wanting" (91). In her assessment of their porridge, in her testing of their chairs, and in her occupation of their beds, Goldilocks knows what is just right for her, and she claims it. Rose compliments Goldilocks by explaining that "If this is a tale of an outsider searching for identity, then Goldilocks is the first heroine of a fairy tale impelled by her own curiosity, embarking on her own voyage of discovery, braving her own dangers, and rescuing herself" (92). Goldilocks certainly appears ahead of Brown's child bunny character in the process of individuation, but it is this growing independence that may explain why Brown and Hurd included allusions to the folktale in their picture book.

Each of the objects that Goldilocks tests in her story surfaces in *My World.* Most subtly, the porridge appears in the bunny family's breakfast scene, in bowls of three on the kitchen table, while the father and child bunnies hold their spoons above their food, ready to test its temperature for themselves. The mother bunny is still busy in the kitchen, stirring a larger bowl at the counter while her porridge waits for her at the table. The chairs and the beds are more explicitly addressed, the bunny child narrator making clear in each scene that he has a specific piece of furniture just for him, a separate piece from his parents': "Mother's chair. / My chair [...] My bed. / Mother's bed." In these particular scenes, he makes a distinction between himself and his mother, specifically. Regardless, the references to these objects offer allusions to "Goldilocks." These allusions appear incased in a "Here and Now" story, as influenced by Lucy Sprague Mitchell and her New York Bank Street School of Education:

> Mitchell's firm stance on children's literature in the 1920s was characterized by the emphatically modern urban setting of the *Here and Now Story Book*'s pieces.

> Much of the children's literature of the period remained rooted in nineteenth-century Romanticism, with its idealized imagery of the happy child at home in harmonious natural surroundings. In stark contrast, Mitchell's stories about sky scrapers and airplanes, tugboats and trolleys acknowledged the demographic and social reality that in 1921 the majority of American children lived in cities.
>
> (Marcus *Margaret* 53)

Mitchell's perspective on best topics for children's narratives stood in stark contrast to the leading purveyors of children's literature at the time—librarians. In particular, Anne Carroll Moore, head children's librarian of the New York Public Library from 1906–1941, championed fairy tales and fantasy for children, and she densely populated her library's bookshelves with such titles. Brown biographer Marcus Leonard explains,

> the librarian was a moral idealist who regarded childhood as a fixed state of innocence to be shielded from, rather than shaped by, historical change and environmental factors [...] Mitchell, for her part, was convinced that people like Moore lived in a sentimental dreamworld.
>
> (*Margaret* 57)

What became known as the "fairy tale war" between the educators and librarians strongly impacted Margaret Wise Brown, who studied under Mitchell but didn't necessarily adhere as tenaciously to the Here and Now campaign as her mentor did. Marcus considers,

> *Goodnight Moon* is a here-and-now story, but one so supercharged with emotion, with so freewheeling a sense of the fantastic as an aspect of the everyday, as to render it a cunning transparency of Bank Street ideas and their opposites. Margaret's simple-sounding bedtime story was her most incisive response to the old Fairy Tale War.
>
> (Marcus *Margaret* 189)

As *Goodnight Moon*'s prequel, however, *My World* may do an even better job of responding to the War by blending a here-and-now story in which the child protagonist explores his concrete reality with an old folktale, creating with the two approaches a readable, enjoyable text for children. In yet this additional aspect of *My World*, Brown continues to emphasize philosophical exploration of the child's world.

The book's ending registers success in separation-individuation, if not specifically completion of the process, as well as blends realism and fantasy. The final full-color spread shows the bunny child swinging in his yard as his parents remain enclosed by the house's front porch. The text reads, "Your world. / My world. / I can swing / Right over the world."

Not only is the child physically separated from his parents in this illustration, he is also placed outside the domestic building, close to the family car and in front of a distant train pictured heading over a hill. These modes of transportation, as well as the driveway which stretches into the unknown distance, represent the possibility of movement away from home, access to a bigger world, and methods of departure. In addition, the bunny child vocalizes a difference between "Your" world and his own; he realizes that objects, space, and time do not only rely on subjective experience, but our entire worlds may constitute separate, individual places. His triumph in understanding this truth appears in the celebratory claim that he can "swing / Right over the world." He has mastered his world; he has mastered his perspective; he is capable of fantastic feats. This ending suggests to child readers that philosophical analysis can lead to psychological achievement.

Such picture books as *My World* demonstrate the artistry of many of Brown's books, not only in writing but also in visual art and the Modern philosophies engaged by the two. Brown's collaboration with Leonard Weisgard in *Red Light, Green Light* (1944), for example, combines dreamlike, surreal visuals with considerations of social conformity and semiotic theory. These narratives treat themes of individuality and belonging through Modern artifacts of philosophical inquiry—for children. This exposure extends, however, even outside of her individual texts. Margaret Wise Brown's tragic early death at the age of forty-two did not rob children of quality nor quantity of her work, considering the number of texts she had already published as well as the plans she left for future publications. Brown left a legacy in 1952 that contributed to her depiction of the child as retaining "complete authority [...] Everything in [Brown's] universe revolves around the child as a central 'human' presence, and this presence names its universe" (Stanton 71). Unknowingly, Brown left behind an additional

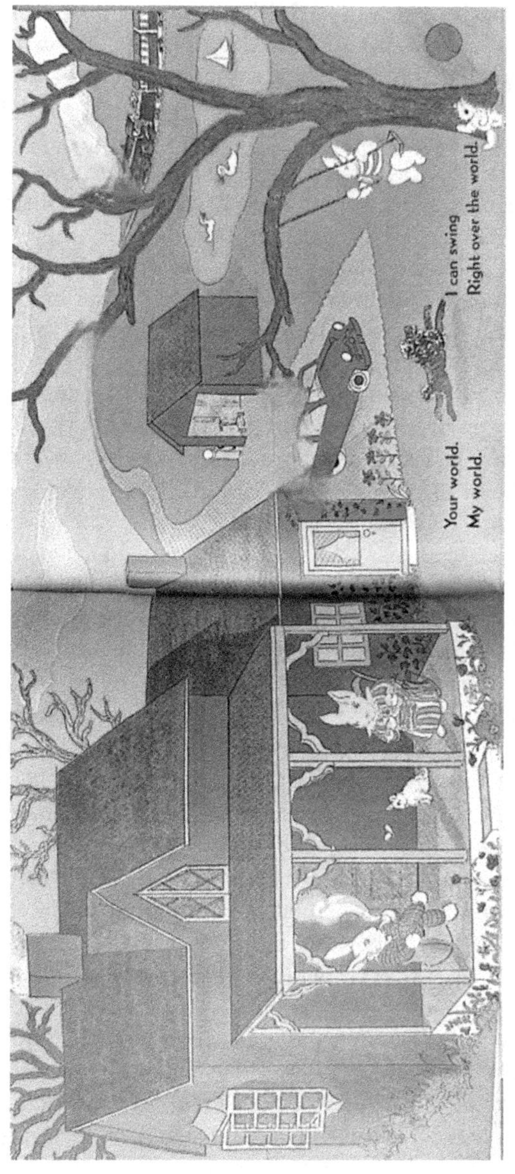

Figure 3.2 Brown, Margaret Wise. *My World.* HarperCollins, 1949. pp. 30–31.

experience that provides child readers with the potential to understand and to prioritize themselves further, a thematic goal her previously published texts had already established. Margaret Wise Brown's publication legacy allows her readers to access temporality, or the unity of time, which Martin Heidegger argues is necessary to understand the self. Through experience with her oeuvre, readers have the opportunity to develop their most authentic selves.

Between 1937, when Brown's first book, *When the Wind Blew*, was published, and December of 1952, when an embolism suddenly ended her life, Brown proved herself a prolific author. Reprints, international publications, new editions, and generic revisions make any specific count of Brown's oeuvre very difficult, but biographers agree that, during her lifetime, Brown completed over ninety picture books, adaptations, translations, magazine stories, articles, and essays, published with nine American publishers, and collaborated with thirty-four illustrators (Marcus "Margaret" 54). Unlike many authors, Brown "lived to see her books become extremely popular," particularly *The Little Fur Family* (1946), *Goodnight Moon* (1947), and *The Runaway Bunny* (1942) (Marcus *Margaret* 2). Her books have continued to appear since 1953, even though in smaller amounts than those published while she still lived. According to the Library of Congress's records, twenty-one additional stories appeared under her name throughout the rest of the 1950s. Some of these might have been texts already in the publishing pipeline, which would explain why Harper, Little Golden Books, and William R. Scott remained Brown's most frequent publishers through the rest of that decade. Those twenty-one stories also usually featured the visual artists with whom she had collaborated previously. For example, artwork by Jean Charlot, Tibor Gergely, Clement Hurd, Esphyr Slobodkina, Leonard Weisgard, and Garth Williams makes new appearances. The 1950s also see illustrations contributed by Crockett Johnson and Richard Scarry, possibly in tribute to Brown's lasting contributions. The 1960s and 1970s, however, fail to represent Brown well, as only four texts of hers appeared in the 1960s, two of which were published by her friend Scott, and only one text was published in the 1970s. These decades, in addition to the 1980s with only three more stories published, mark the natural decline of a deceased author who no longer writes new material. When publisher Amy Gary discovered a trunk of unpublished Margaret Wise Brown manuscripts in the barn attic of Brown's sister, Roberta, in 1990, interest in Brown suddenly reemerged, however. Thirteen new titles appeared throughout the 1990s, including three stories Brown had written for Walt Disney. Since 2000, another forty-six new Margaret Wise Brown stories have found publication, numbers much closer to her prolific output while still living. In addition, these counts don't include adaptations to new media, new editions, or reprints of texts she published herself. Those lists mirror the new publications in tapering off until the 1990s, when they reappeared in large numbers, at least sixty-three since 2000. Now that Brown has gained a second shelf-life, it raises the question why she is still popular, since "over half a century later, her light is burning ever brighter" (Gary xii). Among the many answers to this question falls the philosophy of time; with Margaret Wise Brown's death, this author created the potential for her readers to experience temporality, another avenue for her child readers to engage with philosophical ideas.

Many philosophers have spent great effort in trying to understand time, including Aristotle, Kant, Hegel, and Henri Bergson. St. Augustine's *Confessions*, however, explores the concept of time along avenues that illuminate Margaret Wise Brown's impact in interesting ways. *Confessions*, philosophers often agree,

> for the first time in the history of Western Philosophy sets forth the problem of time and surveys it in its full scope. If, Augustine argues, the present becomes a determination of time, a temporal aspect, only by flowing into the past, how can we speak of a being that subsists only by destroying itself?
>
> (Cassirer 166)

Augustine's problem with time stemmed from an impossibility he recognized in conceiving of time as a temporal flow. This flow constitutes continual, permanent change that cannot be understood as a being itself or as derived from a being. If this is the case, time is not an entity that we can understand objectively; there is nothing definite or objective about it. For that reason, Augustine moves the definition of time from the objective to a subjective experience. In order for us to understand what Augustine calls our "Being-in-the-present," or the condition of possibility of knowledge, we can no longer relate ourselves to the impossibility of objective time. He explains,

> it is now quite clear that neither future nor past actually exists. Nor is it right to say there are three times, past, present and future. Perhaps it would be more correct to say: there are three times, a present of things past, a present of things present, a present of things future. For these three exist in the mind, and I find them nowhere else.
>
> (Augustine 233, book 11, xx)

For Augustine, no longer can humans understand time as three distinct and objective beings, instead, "This switch from a triality of substances to a triality of 'directions' departing from the now, implies a switch from objective to subjective time" (Froeyman 67). Time now exists as subjective experience, or what Augustine calls "the impress produced in [our minds] by things as they pass and abiding in you when they have passed: and it is present" (223, book 11, xx). The present is the only measurable, experiential time available to us, and even that measure only exists within subjective, mental perception. This leaves Augustine to place value only on "being in the present (which we might call 'experience')" (Froeyman 71). His new conceptions of time in this way and the value moved from objective, measurable time to subjective, individual, present-based experience influenced much of Western philosophy on the subject.

St. Augustine's queries about time reappear in Martin Heidegger's influential work *Being and Time* (1927/1962), described as "one of the most important philosophical works of modern times" (Carman xiii). This German philosopher took Augustine's emphasis on Being-in-the-present and conceived of it as a unity of time, what he calls Temporality:

> Time must be brought to light—and genuinely conceived—as the horizon for all understanding of Being and for any way of interpreting it. In order for us to discern this, *time* needs to be *explicated primordially as the horizon for the understanding of Being, and in terms of temporality as the Being of Dasein, which understands Being.*
>
> (Heidegger 39, italics in original)

Time retains great value for Heidegger because it allows us to understand Being, and his particular conception of time is that of a unity: "According to Heidegger, temporality is a unity against which past, present and future stand out as ecstasies while remaining essentially interlocked" (Wheeler 2.3.3 par. 2). Temporality is human experience of time in the present, including experience of past and future in memory and anticipation. Michael Wheeler explains,

> Heidegger is concerned not with clock-time (an infinite series of self-contained nows laid out in an ordering of past, present and future) or with time as some sort of relativistic phenomenon that would satisfy the physicist. Time thought of in either of these ways is a present-at-hand phenomenon.
>
> (2.3.3 par. 2)

This is where Augustine's influence surfaces as both philosophers prioritize subjective experience in the present over objective entities of past and future.

This unity, or temporality, matters most, according to Heidegger, because of the possibility it allows us to understand ourselves. Heidegger terms "the being that defines the entity we are" Dasein, and his work seeks to interrogate the entity of Dasein within temporality (Carman xv). He encourages us to "ask ourselves, that is, how we experience and understand ourselves and the world around us, or more precisely how we experience and understand our *being* and the being of all the things we take *to be*" (Carman xv, italics in original). To analyze Dasein is to analyze human subjective experience. This analysis has to take place within temporality, and Heidegger takes Augustine's present of things past, present of things present, and present of things future and assigns each a particular dimension of temporality that is primary toward which Dasein orients itself. Heidegger explains,

> The unity of the horizontal schemata of future, Present, and having been, is grounded in the ecstatical unity of temporality […] With one's factical Being-there, a potentiality-for-Being is in each case projected in the horizon of the future, one's 'Being-already' is disclosed in the horizon of having been, and that with which one concerns oneself is discovered in the horizon of the Present.
>
> (Heidegger 416, par. 365)

Heidegger calls the dimension of the past "thrownness," the world into which we find ourselves having been thrown, an already-present, determined, fatalistic set of structures. His dimension of the present he terms "fallen-ness," consisting of idle talk, curiosity, and ambiguity which obscure the world and create distraction in our recognition of authenticity. "Projection" constitutes Heidegger's dimension of the future, consisting of our options limited by culturally conditioned structures. Each and all of these dimensions, unified, provide our opportunity to understand Dasein, or being. Wheeler explains,

> each event of intelligibility that makes up a 'moment' in Dasein's existence must be unpacked using all three temporal ecstasies. Each such event is constituted by thrownness (past), projection (future) and falling/discourse (present). In a sense, then, each such event transcends (goes beyond) itself as a momentary episode of Being by, in the relevant sense, co-realizing a past and a future along with a present.
>
> (Wheeler 2.3.3 par. 7)

These three dimensions, or horizons, work together in each "episode of Being" to create Heidegger's "care," or sense-making.

Temporality, then, provides the transcendental condition for care or the dimensionality of care, which we create by combining thrownness, projection, and fallen-ness. Considering the world into which we have landed, its limitations and problems, recognizing our current fallen-ness in the distraction that the world provides, and in deciding what we project as we anticipate the future, Heidegger argues, humans have the ability to create authentic or inauthentic selves. An authentic self arises from independent, conscious recognition of temporality and care, resulting in self-chosen qualities of being, while an inauthentic self is a "fallen" self, lost to the decisions of others and mired in the distractions of fallen-ness. Margaret Wise Brown's early death creates a temporality in both the reading of individual texts and in her oeuvre that provides the opportunity for readers to create authentic selves.

The experience of reading an individual Margaret Wise Brown book can play with readers' experiences of time in ways that may lead them to temporality. Take, for instance, Brown's *The Color Kittens*, originally published in 1949 and illustrated by Alice and Martin Provensen. This story has been republished over eight times as an independent book, twice with different illustrators, in both hardcover and soft, once as a book with sound effects, and most recently as a board book. An adult reading the 1994 Little Golden Books edition, illustrated by Kathi Ember, may also, in the present of that experience, re-experience through memory a past reading of the original 1949 Little Golden Book edition, illustrated by Alice and Martin Provensen, and project through anticipation a future experience of reading the 2009 Little Golden Treasures board book edition. This moment of temporality through *The Color Kittens* may strongly appeal to a reader, providing a reason to continue to return to Brown's text and the potential for Heidegger's sense-making. This experience would differ from a simple re-reading of any literature with the expectation of reading the text again in the future because of the reinterpretations of Brown's work. This example is not simply a repeated experience; it is a triality of similar but essentially different experiences all located in the present yet perceived through subjective care. The thrownness of the "present of things past" could provide the awareness of limitations on the reader's life that precipitated change in her character since that remembered moment. The projection of the "present of things future" may contribute a feeling of freedom in the knowledge that there are still choices to be made, and the balance of these two dimensions would constitute a clearer understanding of "the formally existential totality of Dasein's ontological structural whole" (Heidegger 237). The three distinct "horizons" allow the present reading to surpass a "momentary episode of Being" by allowing for greater authenticity by "co-realizing a past and a future along with a present" (Wheeler 2.3.3 par. 7). Margaret Wise Brown's continual publication provides multiple opportunities for such self-recognition as many other stories such as *The Big Red Barn* (1956, 1985, 1989), *The Diggers* (1960, 1995, 1998), *The Golden Egg Book* (1947, 1975, 1999, 2004, 2015), and *Nibble Nibble: Poems for Children* (1959, 1986, 2007) have enjoyed multiple editions and retellings.

Not only do readings of individual Brown books provide experience with temporality, but the author's oeuvre as a whole also mirrors this episode. On the one hand, readers may quickly assume a familiarity with what defines Brown's historical books as opposed to her unpublished manuscripts. As Matthew Turner breezily remarks in his semiotic analysis of Brown's most famous bedtime story, "*Goodnight Moon* is gently but clearly relegated to a place in the past" (75). This clarity he expects, however, is complicated again by the many reprintings, retellings, and parodies that *Goodnight Moon* has inspired. Leonard Marcus explains,

> In fifteen or so years, from 1937 to 1952, Brown produced a formidable library of more than ninety picture books and story and poetry collections for children. She did not, unfortunately perhaps for biographers, always publish these in the order of their writing. For although she wished her work brought out quickly, [...] Brown at any one time was likely to be writing ten or twenty different stories; there is no way to tell from the manuscripts which ones were set aside for years and which ones finished immediately.
> (Marcus "Margaret" 54)

Not only did Brown's creation of art refuse plotting on any kind of objective, linear timeline, but its experience by readers now continues the refusal. Brown's opus both individually and collectively has appeared, continues to appear, and is guaranteed to continue to appear in a fully present experience. Therefore, encountering Brown's work constitutes a unity of time, a temporality, that provides the condition for sense-making, most particularly an understanding of our existential totalities with the potential for authentic self-making.

In reading Margery Williams's *The Velveteen Rabbit* (1922) through the lenses of Heidegger and D.W. Winnicott, Kirsten Jacobson points out that, for Heidegger, "we are the meaning-givers that make the world possible" (10). The possibility for creation and improvement to this world and to our beings is present, accessible through temporality and openness, "the openness to novel possibilities of meaning that is revealed in play [...] As Heidegger suggests, our true maturity or authenticity lies in such an openness" (Jacobson 11). Margaret Wise Brown often provides this possibility for creating meaning, for creating sense, for maturity and authenticity. She challenged readers and addressed children in her books in ways that continue to allow them to process their own philosophical development, to transcend episodic moments of present, and she unknowingly, through her publishing and untimely death, allowed them these moments in temporality. Through her representation of human relationship to objects, to psychological growth, to conceptions of time and how those conceptions engender authentic selves, Brown respected children and their ability to entertain nuanced self-development. Readers may return to Brown for what they think is a continued childhood experience, for the sharing of childhood narratives with new generations, for nostalgia, but they may also return for an unrecognized opportunity for sense-making, for greater understanding of subjective being.

Note

1 Here, Marcus compares the child bunny's ever broader, wider, and more encompassing addresses to Brown's own use of pseudonyms in her work, which he postulates as an experiment in "chang[ing] oneself" (*Margaret* 156).

References

Augustine. *Confessions*, translated by F.J. Sheed. Hackett, 1942.

Brown, Margaret Wise. *Goodnight Moon*, illustrated by Clement Hurd. Harper, 1947.

———. *My World*, illustrated by Clement Hurd. Harper, 1949.

———. *Red Light, Green Light*, illustrated by Leonard Weisgard. Doubleday, 1944.

———. *The Little Fur Family*, illustrated by Garth Williams. Harper 1946.

Carman, Taylor. "Foreword." *Being and Time*, translated by John MacQuarrie and Edward Robinson. Harper Perennial, 2008, pp. xiii–xxi.

Cassirer, Ernst. *The Philosophy of Symbolic Forms. Volume 3: The Phenomenology of Knowledge*, translated by Ralph Manheim. Yale UP, 1957.

Costello, Peter. *Philosophy in Children's Literature*. Rowman and Littlefield, 2011.

Dainton, Barry, "Temporal Consciousness." *The Stanford Encyclopedia of Philosophy* (Winter2016 Edition), edited by Edward N. Zalta. https://plato.stanford.edu/archives/ win2016/entries/consciousness-temporal/.

Estes, Angela M. "Margaret Wise Brown: Awakened by You Know Who." *Children's Literature*, 22, 1994, pp. 162–70.

Falcon, Andrea. "Aristotle on causality." *Stanford Encyclopedia of Philosophy*. Metaphysics Research Lab, Department of Philosophy, Stanford University, 2008.

Froeyman, Anton. "Anticipation and the Constitution of Time in the Philosophy of Ernst Cassirer." *International Journal of Computing Anticipatory Systems*, 23, 2010, pp. 64–73.

Gary, Amy. *In the Great Green Room: The Brilliant and Bold Life of Margaret Wise Brown*. Flatiron, 2016.

Heidegger, Martin. *Being and Time*, translated by John MacQuarrie and Edward Robinson. Harper Perennial, 1962.

Jacobson, Kirsten. "Heidegger, Winnicott, and The Velveteen Rabbit: Anxiety, Toys, and the Drama of Metaphysics." *Philosophy in Children's Literature*, edited by Peter Costello. Lexington Books, 2012, pp. 1–20.

Janiak, Andrew. "Kant's Views on Space and Time." *Stanford Encyclopedia of Philosophy*. Metaphysics Research Lab, Department of Philosophy, Stanford University, 2010.

Mahler, Margaret S., Fred Pine & Anni Bergman. *The Psychological Birth of the Human Infant: Symbiosis and Individuation*. Basic Books, 1975.

Marcus, Leonard S. *Margaret Wise Brown: Awakened by the Moon*. Beacon, 1992.

———. "Margaret Wise Brown." *Dictionary of Literary Biography: American Writers for Children, 1900–1960*, edited by John Cech, vol. 22. Bruccoli Clark, 1983, pp. 42–70.

Opie, Iona & Peter Opie, editors. *Classic Fairy Tales*. Oxford UP, 1974.

Pine, Fred. "Preface." *The Psychological Birth of the Human Infant: Symbiosis and Individuation*, edited by Margaret S. Mahler, Fred Pine & Anni Bergman. Basic Books, 2000, pp. vii–xiii.

Rose, Oliver. "Whatever Became of Goldilocks?" *Frontiers: A Journal of Women Studies*, 2, 3, 1977, pp. 85–93.

Stanton, Joseph. "'Goodnight Nobody': Comfort and the Vast Dark in the Poems in Margaret Wise Brown and her Collaborators." *The Lion and the Unicorn*, 14, 2, 1990, pp. 66–76.

Turner, Matthew R. "Goodnight, *Goodnight Moon*: A Semiotic Analysis of Berkeley Breathed's *Goodnight Opus*." *Interdisciplinary Humanities*, 29, 1, 2012, pp. 67–76.

Wheeler, Michael. "Martin Heidegger." *The Stanford Encyclopedia of Philosophy*, edited by Edward N. Zalta. 2016, https://plato.stanford.edu/archives/win2016/entries/heidegger/.

Wolfs, Bailey. "The Psychoanalytic Milieu of Margaret Mahler: Historical and Contemporary Perspectives on the Separation-Individuation Process." *WUPJ*, 10, September 2022, pp. 1–11.

4 The Musical Artist

Perhaps the most Modern characteristic of Margaret Wise Brown's picture books is a strain she dabbled in from the beginning but only fully engaged in during the very last years of her life—music. While Brown's earliest publications incorporated elements of lyrical language and experimentation with sound, her last years saw her forming plans with such artists as Burl Ives and signing contracts with record companies to begin applying her writing talent to music for children. At the time, in the late 1940s and early 1950s, music had achieved highest status as an art form among the Modernists.[1] Its ability to express emotion, to emulate reality, even to effect social change caused composers such as Richard Wagner, philosophers such as Arthur Schopenhauer, and writers such as Ezra Pound to call for the inclusion of music into other artistic disciplines, to engage in fulfillment of synesthesia. Margaret Wise Brown began to answer this call. In addition to Brown's playful, genre-crossing writing style, her partnerships with experimental visual artists, as well as her incorporation of childhood development theories, her participation in Modernism surfaces in the value of music expressed by many of her books. Through her picture books about sound and music, her narratives translated into music, and especially her emphasis on intermediality, or melopoetics, Brown joins the ranks of Modernists in her own genre of children's books while prioritizing representations of children's subjectivity.[2]

Long before Brown, writers considered the lyrical opportunities in words. *The Oxford English Dictionary* records the first use of "prosody" in English as occurring near 1475 to refer to elements of grammar, particularly rhythm and sound, in pronunciation of words. This general use later grew more specific in its reference to meter in

DOI: 10.4324/9781032727028-5

verse and the employment of literary devices. By the early twentieth century, however, Ezra Pound began using the term by returning to its roots in ancient Greek to describe words accompanied by music and/or their necessary syllabic accents, whether in poetry or prose. In this application, Pound expresses the writer's acknowledgment that language is often musical in nature. In fact, Modernist scholar Tim Armstrong explains that "Pound also insists that poetry must learn from music a multisensory rhythmic complexity so that it 'becomes not only aware of that given form, but more sensitive to other forms, rhythms, defined planes, or masses'" (121). Pound was not alone in valorizing the emphasis of musicality in writing. Earlier in 1861, in his essay "Richard Wagner et 'Tannhäuser' á Paris," Charles Baudelaire also encouraged critics to recognize that writers often "aimed toward musicality" both for the pleasing sound that aim produces and for the freedom from constraint that music lends expression. This shift in the meaning of the word "prosody" from grammar to intentional musicality parallels a growing interest around the turn of the century among writers in the ways that music already informed writing and the new ways it could more deeply engage it.

On the other side of the conversation, musicians and theorists had long recognized the ways that music serves as communication. First, many viewed it as able to express individual emotions. Then, the eighteenth century in particular saw changes in thinking about instrumental music specifically. Arthur Schopenhauer, for one, wrote of music's ability to communicate essences, for "with no vocal parts and therefore no narratives that could be used to reinforce dominant ideologies, it appeared to offer a pure form of communication, distinct from language or reasoning which usually mediates experience" (Moss 33). Thinking of music as another form of communication brought to writers' attention the possibilities of breaking free from the constraints of words and their limitations in meaning; this understanding meant that music could transcend language, could transcend many of the classical arts, even as it continued to share "concepts and emotions of distinctly human importance" (Moss xiii). Writers remain masters of words, however, and they were not arguing to abandon the art of letters but instead to begin thinking of ways of integrating the two disciplines, a seemingly natural integration considering the focus on prosody already present in writing.

German philosopher and musicologist Theodor Adorno was, perhaps, most clearly able to express the possibilities of communication present in musical compositions. In his 1956 essay "Music, Language, and Composition," for instance, Adorno makes a distinction between language and music clear by referencing the ways that music can avoid the tension inherent in semiotics. He argues,

> music resembles language in the sense that it is a temporal sequence of articulated sounds which are more than just sounds. They say something, often something human [...] But what has said cannot be detached from the music. Music creates no semiotic system.
>
> (401; ellipses in original)

Since music exists as a single system, there is no chaffing present between the sign and the signified, as necessarily remains in language use. Therefore, music can get closer to the essence of an idea, Adorno argues, an essence that Modernists chased after, no longer trusting of traditional voices: "The sonorous gesture of language in modernity seems to tend towards such biblical reunion of words and things, towards the original identity between the sign and what it denotes [...] semiophony aims at the utopia of immediacy" (Derveaux 9). Moving writing closer to music, then, would not only merge artistic mediums, but it might also move nearer the central concepts that artists want to convey.

According to more contemporary musicologists such as Marc Derveaux, the particular elements in literature that bridge music and writing are "semiophonic objects." These "phrastic elements, expressive features, acoustical characteristics of speech [...] belong to the spoken-sung figure [and] hesitate indefinitely between vocal art and simple speech" (7, 5). Semiophony, then, is a moment when the written word moves into song and back again. Building these moments into any length can result in intermediality, crossroads between modern artistic forms, or, even more specifically, melopoeia—crossroads where words carry musical properties.[3] This melopoeia is how many Modernists found possibility for expression and how Margaret Wise Brown primarily experimented musically in her books.

The two central reasons that Modern authors were interested in melopoeia, in incorporating elements of music into writing, were for its greater access to expression and an interest in synesthesia, or of using one artistic discipline to express a different one.[4] First, those authors who found themselves attracted to the new, to experimentation, to creating original forms often used writing to demonstrate its own boundaries, to play with non-linguistic "rhythms and structures to achieve unusual forms that contribute to the aesthetic complexity of their literature" (Moss x). Some writing demoted the meaning of words in the promotion of letter sound and syllabic emphasis for the purpose of representing the failures of language to express meaning fully. Gertrude Stein's *Tender Buttons* (1914), for example, often relies on combinations of word pronunciation rather than on the signs accompanying the words themselves.[5] But in a larger sense, Modernists reached beyond simple critiques of language to try new combinations for the ways they demonstrated new ways of thinking. They found greater interest in using all available means of expression for their opening of cognitive possibilities. Scholar Gemma Moss explains,

> Closely connected to the crisis of language, the ideas and formal innovations driven by music participate in longstanding investigations of commonsense thinking and rational thought. Music can create meaning without referring to anything outside itself and it also works directly on the body: it vibrates the organism and seems to affect the senses without the mediation of language, or even before a response to it has been rationalized. Music in modernist literature is often used to re-energise and reshape language, or bring individual perception and interpretation into the foreground.
>
> (Moss 1)

Hope of reaching further in capturing truth on a page than words might allow, interest in devising new ways of thinking, and even grounding artistic experience in the body all drew Modernists toward melopoetics.[6]

Second, in the wake of decades of mounting Modern Temper, Modernism also developed a predilection for the unity of artistic effort. Scholars often cite Richard Wagner's 1865 performance of *Tristan und Isolde* as the birthplace of Modern synesthesia in music, capped in the orchestra pit by Igor Stravinsky's *The Rite of Spring* in 1913. Wagner's influence on Modernism came primarily from his idea of the *Gesamtkunstwerk*, a utopian, universal artwork that might bridge artistic disciplines to provide "an absorbing aesthetic experience" that would leave an audience more socially aware (Moss 9). This idea included matching set designs and colors to the colors Wagner saw expressed in his music and associating certain operatic characters with visual cues such as light, echoed by the instruments that introduce those characters. Armstrong calls Wagner's attempts a "dynamic multimedia mapping of the senses," indicating the overlapping of artistic methods to create a richer, more expressive final product (120). And these efforts explain why music became a leading discipline in Modernism, as it wasn't until decades later that literary artists took up similar goals. While high Modernist literary experimentation burgeoned for adult readers, Margaret Wise Brown created moments of melopoeia, synesthesia, and experimented with semiophony for a child audience, using these devices to express a child's experience of the world.

Brown began experimenting with sounds and semiophony with her early *Noisy Book* series. Although these books did not concern music directly, they focused on sound as interpretation of reality, imbued with meaning. The premise of the books follows Muffin the dog who gets a cinder in his eye in the first story. In order to encourage healing, the doctor puts a bandage over Muffin's eyes for the remainder of the day, and he can no longer see; "But Muffin could hear." As Muffin goes about his day, the narrator lists the sounds that Muffin can hear and the onomatopoeic representation of each sound: "Bzzzzzz bzzzzzz / a bee / Swishhhh swishhh / car wheels / Chirp chirp / a bird." Leonard Weisgard contributes illustrations to each page that often depict the object Muffin hears, but each object is encased in a shape that also attempts to mimic the sound within. The hissing radiator appears in a squiggly border that visually reaches to capture the "s" sound. The veterinarian's sneeze appears in a sharp, angled shape that links the short bursts of a sneeze with the visual equivalent of abrupt, sudden changes in sound and volume. Moss explains that many Modernists "were deeply influenced by the newly dissonant music of the early twentieth century that registered the sounds of material existence: industrial machinery, city life, and mechanized warfare" (x–xi). Likewise, as Muffin leaves the doctor, he hears the sounds of city life—men hammering, horns blowing, a firetruck passing, people's feet walking. Muffin does not experience melodic song, but his story points to the sounds that fill the real, Modern world, the world even of children. As Armstrong points out, "The drive here is towards a synthesis of different senses and artistic modes" (121). Brown's picture book provides the perfect place to practice this Modern art.

Brown's first *Noisy Book* was so successful that she continued to collaborate with Weisgard to create them, placing each story in a different location that included new sounds for Muffin to explore. These sounds certainly typify "ordinary, commonplace experience: it focuses on [the] concern to defamiliarize the everyday by giving it the kind of attention we often fail to" (Maude 11–12). But for a child readership, the defamiliarization aims less to emphasize ignored experience and more to acknowledge perceived experience. Brown could both create texts that followed Modernist tendencies and books that portray subjective child experience, as they often overlap. This practice continued even into such metaphysical considerations as appear in *The Quiet Noisy Book* (1950). In this story, Muffin wakes to a very quiet sound, and he spends the book guessing what that sound might have been. His ideas include butter melting, a skyscraper scraping the sky, and a fish breathing. These possibilities, of course, posit actions that do not make discernable sound, encouraging readers to question the very premise of the exercise. But these impossibilities work in several ways. First, they stimulate consideration of what sound consists of, how it is made, and whether it can happen without a receptive ear. Second, they "defamiliarize the everyday" by providing space for readers to stop and consider the possibilities of experiencing life with every sense. Third, they engage in the art of synesthesia, representing audible (or not so audible) moments in word, art, and spoken expression if the book is read aloud. Although not examples of traditional music, the *Noisy Books* constitute intermediality.

In 1946, Horace Grenell started Young People's Records as a competitor to Disney's music for children. Grenell's genius blossomed in his idea to create a subscription service for families so that they could acquire new records each month, based on popular stories, folktales, and folk music (Bonner 3–6). Horace Grenell's wife, Judith Sidorsky, worked as a pianist and a music teacher at the Bank Street School of Education at the time, and her work inspired Grenell to provide children with music and "audio plays"—narrative recordings with sound effects and musical interludes—that represented real life, in contrast to Disney's fairy tale fare (Bonner 6). Unsurprisingly, a number of these records quickly contained Margaret Wise Brown stories. In fact, most of Brown's contributions to Young People's Records were her *Noisy Book* stories, and historian David Bonner even suggests that *Muffin Could Hear* was "probably the first story-based record ever made for the preschool child" (Bonner 65). In this case, not only was

Brown creating Modern art in her books about sound, but she also collaborated on ground-breaking auditory experiences for children. Unfortunately, Brown's relationship with the record company often grew unsettled as many of her stories required quiet reflection, and YPR's aim encouraged active engagement. In order to fit her stories to the new medium, changes to Brown's stories appeared in the audio versions, and "Brown herself was not as impressed, expressing dissatisfaction with four of the first five YPR adaptations of her work" (Bonner 65–66). She continued to license her narratives with the company, however, until her death. The book adaptation she seemed most pleased with, according to Bonner, was one of her most successful tales about music, *The Little Brass Band.*

In her article for the 1952 volume of *The Book of Knowledge*, Brown explained,

> A good picture-book story clearly shows its musical origin, for it can almost be whistled. I am speaking of the cadence and lilt that carries the story along from page to page. […] [These stories] all have their own melodies behind the storytelling. When such stories are told well, really told, their cadence and rhythm are a large part of their meaning.
>
> ("Stories" 166)

Brown's biographer, Leonard Marcus, attributes this predilection for prosody to her appreciation of Modern women artists and educators (*Margaret* 257). Regardless, so many of Brown's books stand as examples and experiments in synesthesia that her admiration of this crossroads clearly surfaces. For instance, *The Little Brass Band* (1948) tells the story of a medieval musical troupe who gather to serenade a village instrumentally, the theme of the story valorizing community and unity. The book opens with the music of a rooster who wakes the narrative with his onomatopoeic call to rise, sound captured in letters, followed by two pages that describe the band assembling, but the narration attributes this action to the instruments themselves, not their players. The focus stays on the music, not even recognizing any people: "Early in the morning, the little brass band came over the hill, one by one. First the trumpet from a distant farm / Then the trumpet was joined by the drum in the valley." Although Clement Hurd depicts the players on the third page, they appear tiny, dwarfed by the visual weight of the bassoon on the left side of the page. However, it is interesting to note that the three players appear in the center of two roads that create an X, as the text narrates, "And along came the trumpet and the drum to the crossroads, where the big bassoon was waiting." This written story, expressed with visual art, concerning music includes a literal crossroads. As two "golden horns" add to the band on the following page, the French horns overlap one another, linked, joined, as one of the paths from the crossroads carries over the page gutter and runs behind them, including them in the group. As readers turn the page, the road continues in the background behind "a flute, a clarinet, and an oboe," the original musicians again distant figures down the side of the page. Brown's synesthetic metaphors continue yet again as readers then learn that the three new instruments "were waiting on the bridge." This literal and metaphorical bridge completes the band just as it provides the means for linking the artistic disciplines represented by the book.

At this point in the story, the plot shifts to describing the union of people that the band inspires. This music brings disparate types into community, from the most innocuous sleeping baby to the significant and essential police chief, culminating in a town square concert where "the people came and lay in the grass and listened." The concert represents converging of individuals, of lives, but also of art. Children's book scholar Barbara Badar explains that Margaret Wise Brown "was launched on the songs and musical stories; and the best of the musical stories, *The Little Brass Band*, was performed publicly as well as recorded, and later became a book" (264). This brief story demonstrates expression of Modern intermediality through its content, as Armstrong points out that mixing of artistic forms "can appear within the work's reality or inform its modes of writing and representation" (119). Brown's books about music provide important examples of this Modern experiment.

Contrasting *The Little Brass Band*, Brown's book *Love Song of the Little Bear* (2001), also separately published identically under the title *Long Time That I've Loved You* (2020), centrally concerns music, but it is not nearly as successful at representing Modernist tendencies of artistic unity. For one, the narrative itself remains unclear, possibly because of the obscurity that the bear's song lends his meaning. The narrative begins, "By the clear waters / One morning in May, / A little bear was singing / A song that seemed to say: / It's a long time that I've loved you, / Never, never go away." From the book's title and its third line, readers know that the little bear is singing a song.

However, the fourth line complicates the song; it indicates that the song is interpreted by a listener, and the interpretation is not literal—it only "seems" to mean what the book records. The interpretation also remains unclear. Even if the little bear thinks it has loved someone for a long time, its short life proves otherwise, and why is it afraid that the object of its love is going to leave? The story does not answer these questions. The illustrations attempt to fill in some of the narrative gaps, but because the book was published posthumously, Brown herself was not involved in choosing the illustrator or collaborating on illustrations. Therefore, the illustrations represent an interpretation of Brown's story by another party, a situation that many picture books endure, but one that Margaret Wise Brown books published during her lifetime did not experience, due to her concentrated collaboration with the artists who worked on her publications. Katy Hudson provided the artwork for Brown's *Love Song* in this case, and her pictures interpret the song as occurring between a baby bear and an adult bear. The two appear together on most double-paged spreads, often embracing, gazing fondly at each other, and once looking out at the wider world. In this interpretation, Hudson constructs a story around a little bear who wants to explore the big world present outside its nuclear relationship, but the bear also needs the assurance of knowing that, even if it strays, its caregiver will remain present. While this reading makes sense, it does not entirely capture the words' allusions. With the grown bear's presence in the pictures, the song seems much more likely to indicate the adult's thoughts, rather than a child's. The little bear is the one most likely to grow and leave, and the adult is the character who has loved for "a long time." Another likely possibility remains that the song is the adult's imagined translation of the little bear's attitude, that the song's ambiguous message is a result of adult fear and wisdom layered on top of childish behavior, but this possibility depends on Katy Hudson's creation of the adult character. Since that character is never present in the words, Brown could have just as easily have intended the little bear to be singing about nature, the world itself, or the excitement of new experiences.

Half-way through the story, the narrative removes outside perspective: "Spring showers are falling / On waters green and gray. / Beneath the gentle raindrops / There's a little bear at play. / It's a long time that I've loved you, / Never, never go away." Instead of the song seeming to communicate something to an external listener, the narrator now simply provides the context and the song itself. The last page of the book actually moves away from the little bear completely to claim, "That is my little love song, / And all I have to say." At this point, the narrator claims that the song actually expresses the love of yet another presence—the narrator's, the author's, the illustrated parent's—but that question never finds resolution. Both the text of this story and its accompanying illustrations convey vagueness, fear of abandonment, and uncertainty rather than community or union. Song is present, not only in the little bear's song, but in "The birds [...] singing sweetly" and "Every little songbird / Sing[ing] softly on this day." Additionally, the text of the book is written as song, rhyming, carrying rhythm, repeating a refrain, and dividing into verses. Music infuses this story, but the intermediality here fails. The arts do not add to one another but, instead, create gaps and omissions that leave the narrative unfulfilling. A manuscript found in the barn attic of Brown's sister decades following Brown's death, *Love Song* may never have been intended for publication. If it had been published during Brown's lifetime, she certainly would have chosen a more Modern artist to illustrate her work. Regardless, in its present manifestation, this book essentially regards music, yet it does not benefit from the artistic relationships it develops. Surely, under Margaret Wise Brown's direct leadership, this project could have achieved more successful results.

In addition to books that discuss song and music explicitly, there are also those Brown books that were written first as books and then made into music. The first edition of *The Runaway Bunny* (1942) stands as an example of this process as it originally included its own song, "Song of the Runaway Bunny." Margaret Wise Brown wrote the lyrics to this song, and Julien Tiersot arranged the music, but the song was left out of subsequent editions (Susina 121). The song has since been resurrected, however, in a 2021 HBO Max animated special of *The Runaway Bunny*. In this new version, Clement Hurd's illustrations come to life, and such artists as Mariah Carey and Kelly Rowland appear on the soundtrack; Tracee Ellis Ross performs Brown's original lullaby. Brown's 1948 *Wait Till the Moon Is Full* is another example. In this story about a baby raccoon who wants to explore outside of his safe burrow, the child is told over and over by his mother to "wait." This story includes moments of prosody as the mother's response to her child's questions becomes a refrain, repeated nine times: "Wait. Wait till the moon is full." The first couple of times the mother gives her answer, a reader may hear it spoken in prose, but as the story continues, the words seem to move in and out of song at these refrains, in an almost singsong manner. When the child racoon first states, "I want to see a bird fall out of his nest and fly away in the moonlight," the mother answers, "Wait till the moon is full," as a statement. But when the very next two lines repeat the rhythm, it becomes more musical: "And find another little racoon to play with." "Wait," said his mother. "Wait till the moon is full." The repetitive answer grows comforting, pacifying, and even though the little racoon does not get what he wants right away, the answer persuades him to wait. It does not persuade him, however, to stop asking. Rather than repeat herself even more than she already does, "his mother began to sing." Beyond the prosody hinted at in the structure of the mother/child question and response, this Brown book also includes two full songs, the first about "the Night and the Moon," and the second, "another song." These songs are indicated by appearing in italics. The first song describes animal fun at night under the moon in two six-line stanzas and one seven-line stanza. Although rhyme is present, there is no specific rhyme scheme. The second song describes the moon in three-line stanzas composed of rhyming couplets followed by an unrhymed final line, each representing a different color, describing for the listener different appearances of the night and the moon. In this text, the music contributes to the narrative. Brown combines artistic mediums, and it results in a fuller story, but rather than feeling experimental, the context of the conversation between parent and child and the forum of the children's book locates this intermediality in an unaffected space. Prose and poetry, narrative and song often appear mixed and overlapping in childhood places. Brown even recognizes this reality by providing a reason for the mother racoon's song. As the child continues his questioning, "And because his mother couldn't answer all his questions at once, she sang him another song." Children may come across song in the midst of their routine conversations for the rhetorical situations they create for themselves.

The mixing of music with narrative culminates in the moment that the child finally gets the answer he wants. At the end of the story, "the little racoon looked up at his mother and said, 'See here, my big warm mother, can I go now—out in the woods to see the night?'" And his mother's response is not stated as song, but it stands apart in centered text on a new page, imbued with its own rhythm. It does not appear in italics, but it appears as something new, both in format and in content. Is it stated directly as prose? Is it a poem? Is it a song? The text does not provide an answer, but most likely, it is a combination of the three genres, a moment of melopoetics that utilizes alliteration, anaphora, assonance, enjambment, and repetition while summarizing all of the conversation that has preceded this narrative moment and, at last, giving the child racoon permission to explore the night. Modern in execution, *Wait Till the Moon Is Full* smoothly achieves a rewarding experience of melopoetics, largely due to its application of a child's experience. Similarly to *The Little Brass Band*, the musical nature of *Wait Till the Moon Is Full* was emphasized by its inclusion as an audio play on Young People's Records. Like several of Brown's other stories, *Wait* does not appear identically when translated into the musical narrative format, but it does continue to express its themes of pacification, patience, and maturity.

The clearest examples of Brown's melopoetics are her two books of songs, accompanied by music on CDs, published long after her death, in 2014 and 2015. *Goodnight Songs* and *Goodnight Songs: A Celebration of the Seasons* are comprised of songs intended as lullabies. In the introduction to the 2014 publication, editor Amy Gary claims that, before she passed, Brown was realizing "that [children] made up songs about whatever it was they were doing at the time. She wanted to capture that spirit of a child's world in her songs the way she had in stories." The songs in these collections, however, appear intended as stories sung to children as they go to bed rather than songs that represent children's own voices. The songs do tend to remain simple and brief, though. "The Noon Balloon" consists of three distinct stanzas stretched into a six-stanza song through repetition. "Mambian Melody" is five stanzas long, but only two are original work, and "Goat on the Mountain" contains only a single repeated stanza. This brevity could find explanation in the fact that the songs had not been published when Brown died; maybe they weren't intended to be published, maybe they were unfinished, or maybe they are notes and drafts that Sterling Publications repeated to make them song-length. But there is also the possibility that Brown intended this brevity as representative of the songs children write about their daily activities, the songs they live within. Unfortunately, their publication without the participation of Brown herself leaves these possibilities open.

In addition to the contribution of the words themselves, these texts offer illustrations, each song captured visually by a different artist. Successful and talented in their own right, these illustrators voice their inspirations for their contributions in their brief biographies at the end of the books. Some illustrators, such as Bob Staake or Molly Idle, share their respect for the art of Margaret Wise Brown books and their desires to express that respect in their own illustrations: "The bunnies in *Goodnight Moon* are iconic picture book creations. So it was such a treat to have the chance to illustrate my own moonlit, cotton-tailed characters inspired by Margaret Wise Brown" (Idle *Celebration*). Others, such as David Small, explain that their illustrations are interpretations of Brown's stories: "In 'Bunny Jig,' Margaret Wise Brown seems to be poking gentle fun at those who make curious choices of partners in the dance of life. I chose to expand the tale, to make it into a short-short story" (*Celebration*). Still others, such as Sophie Blackall, contributed illustrations that represent the illustrator's current experiences: "[Sophie] recently traveled to India with UNICEF and returned with a head full of peacocks, chattering children, moonlit temples, and patterned saris, all of which inspired her painting for 'Mambian Melody'" (*Goodnight Songs*). With such different voices, styles, and motivations, the artwork of these texts remains quite diverse.

Finally, the music of the *Goodnight Songs* books was contributed by Tom Proutt and Emily Gary. A mixture of folk music and bluegrass, listeners can hear a distant influence of the musical genres appreciated by the progressive educational movement practiced by the Bank Street School and Young Peoples Records. In their notes at the end of each text, Proutt and Gary describe their familiarity with Brown and their intergenerational experiences with her work. They explain that Brown's imagery largely determined the direction of their compositions, and they chose instruments based on the themes of each song:

> The sleepy slide trombone mimics yawning in 'Sleep like a Rabbit.' In 'The Secret Song,' long notes from a bass harmonica create a foghorn effect. These sounds fell into place as we sought to mirror the lovely and lively images in Margaret Wise Brown's poetry.
> (*Goodnight Songs*)

Here, the musicians directly describe the synesthesia they targeted while also labeling Brown's writing as "poetry." Their perspective views the projects as cross-disciplinary artwork, blending poetry, music, and visual art with the express purpose of utilizing synesthesia to inform each medium. With this intent, the *Goodnight Song* books certainly represent a beautiful embodiment of the Modern *Gesamtkunstwerk*. However, the success of the endeavor remains dubious. Necessarily, Brown was not actually aware of this collaboration; some of the artists worked from their own perspectives and experiences while others actively attempted to complement Brown's style, and the musicians often worked from themes or "senses" that they personally felt the words conveyed. Although important contributions to children's literature and art, these texts do not necessarily contribute to Brown's own work as a Modern artist. And maybe that is, now, since her death, an impossible task.

Brown's penchant for rhyming, rhythmic combinations of prose and poetry, as discussed in Chapter 1, could find definition as prose poetry. When considered besides music, these moments could be better described as prosody. But the purposeful combination of multiple artistic areas becomes intermediality, and the purposeful combination of writing and music in particular creates melopoetics. Scholar of music and Modernism, Robert McParland explains that scholars in his discipline "dissolve the boundaries of isolation between academic disciplines while seeking a common cultural legacy [...] they probe a space between the linguistic and the musical that has sometimes been called intermediality or 'melopoetic'" (1). This artistic crossroads describes several of Margaret Wise Brown's books and her dual goals of expressing child subjectivity and offering child readers access to experiences of artistic distinction. Possibly Brown's most highly achieved melopoetic text is *The Golden Sleepy Book* (1948), illustrated by Garth Williams. At first glance, this picture book represents what scholar Julie Jung calls a multi-genre text. While Jung discusses specifically academic writing, she defines a genre common in both literature and scholarship: the combination within a single text of several writing genres, "including poetry, fiction, creative nonfiction, and drama" (33). *The Golden Sleepy Book* consists of three narratives, one poem, one song, two pieces that could be either poems or songs, and a page of sheet music. Jung differentiates between the multi-genre text and what Clifford Geertz calls "blurred genres" by clearly distinguishing between the genres: "Unlike blurred genres, multi-genre texts contain breaks—signified by white space on the printed page—that separate one genre from the next" (33). One of the benefits of multi-genre texts is the way that they blend voices, not simply through including a picture with words (although that certainly has a similar effect), but by writing through each genre in ways that build individual expressions. These techniques create "one type of multivocal discourse where the inclusion of diverse genres adds another layer of 'vocality'" (Jung 33). *The Golden Sleepy Book* moves even farther into expressive attempts most inclusively by experimenting with new art forms and in blending artistic disciplines with the goal of achieving fuller, richer expression. It does so through its unification of textual art, musical art, and visual art.

The Golden Sleepy Book opens with the narrative, "The Whispering Rabbit." In this story, a bunny yawns, but as he opens his mouth wide, a bee flies into his mouth, and he swallows the bee. Initially concerned, he grows even more worried when the bee falls asleep in his throat, and he can only whisper. He finds that he must wake the bee with the quietest sound possible, and with that idea, the story begins to resemble Brown's *Quiet Noisy Book* in the impossible sounds that the rabbit considers. He tries a noise "as quiet as the sound of a bird's wing cutting the air," "the sound of snow falling," "the sound of a bug breathing and a fly sneezing and grass rustling and a fireman thinking." While some of these sounds are familiar, such as grass rustling, others seem entirely impossible; do a fireman's thoughts create sound? In such moments, Brown explores the definitions and boundaries of sound and objective experience. The sound that finally wakes the bee in the bunny's throat is "a little click made hundreds of miles away by a bumblebee in an apple tree in full bloom on a mountaintop. It was the very small click of a bee swallowing some honey from an apple blossom." Not only is this sound difficult to imagine, but it raises the questions of whether it exists and whether a rabbit could imitate it. Additionally, the description of this successful sound appears set apart in the text. It appears in the same font but indented, similar to a block paragraph, in smaller typeface. Often, Brown uses these sorts of shifts in formatting to indicate a move between mediums, but this new paragraph does not look or sound like a poem or a song, the two most likely possibilities. Therefore, it simply indicates something new. This sound does not fit established definitions or expectations. It is itself. Another method that Brown uses to test sound in this story is in her use of onomatopoeia. The bunny's yawn, "Hmmm________," the owl's greeting, "Hooo—hooo—," and even the smaller font size of the lines in which the bunny has to whisper because of the bee's presence all graphically represent sound more explicitly than verbal description would. In this opening story, Brown indicates her interest in the possibilities of sound and the way they can be expressed through text.

The second text in Brown's *Sleepy* book is a poem titled "Rabbit Poem." Interestingly, Clement Hurd's illustration style subtly changes between these texts. Perhaps most clearly, the color palette softens from the more saturated tones in the first narrative to pastels around the poem. The font also moves from a standard text to a stylized title and the poem in italics. Visually, "Rabbit Poem" presents more fancifully. Each of the three stanzas opens with the statement "Nobody knows" and follows by considering "a rabbit's nose," "a rabbit's ears," and "a rabbit's eyes," but Brown does not clearly explain what is not known or who does not know it or even what knowing it would consist of. This thought experiment, like the bunny's sounds in "The Sleepy Rabbit," leaves experience behind and stretches the imagination. Following the poem, *The Golden Sleepy Book* moves back into narrative.

Jung explains, "by refusing to 'fit in' to the conventions of any one genre or subfield, and yet by building alliances with several different genres at once, multigenre texts demand new and better kinds of listening" (xiii). This listening occurs both literally and figuratively in *The Golden Sleepy Book* as it embraces auditory experience as well as profound artistic experience. The following story, "The Dreaming Bunny" constitutes the longest text of the book. In this story, a baby bunny declines to participate with other rabbits in their work and, instead, rests in a cabbage plant, "singing and dreaming and blinking away to himself." His observation saves the community from a fox he notices threatening long before all the busy bunnies think to look up from their work. At this point in the book, Brown has accomplished a multi-genre text. The book has moved from narrative to poetry, back to narrative. Brown has also accomplished intermediality by combining visual art and textual art, not just in tandem, but in dual expression, each medium strengthening the communication of the other. Now, "The Dreaming Bunny" progresses the text into melopoetics. Within the picture book, within the movement between mediums, within this one narrative, Brown includes song. The young bunny protagonist first "makes a dreamy little song to himself about rabbits" and then later "made a song to himself about crows." These two songs appear in the text, set apart by larger indents and italicized font. Like *Wait Till the Moon Is Full*, this story incorporates a third artistic genre within the multi-genre format of the larger picture book, and the third genre concerns music, introducing melopoetics. Interestingly, the second song harkens back to the "Rabbit Poem" by repeating the refrain that "nobody knows." Here, "Nobody knows / Where the red fox goes / Nobody knows / But the wild black crows." But the little bunny knows. He is the one who watches, learns the signs of danger, and shares those signs with the other bunnies. The story teaches readers to appreciate differences among groups. Even though this bunny is named Bunny No Good for his lack of participation, that refusal to work as part of the group saves the group. His difference is necessary for the survival of the community. This theme, expressed by the longest text of the book, finds reflection in the diversity of the art forms communicating it as well. Just as Brown values the individual contributions of song, picture, and word, so too does her story encourage valuing the different contributions of each person.

Fourth in *The Golden Sleepy Book* appears a text that readers could experience as either a poem or a song, "Close Your Eyes." The rhythmic quatrains list animals that all should close their eyes as the day ends and they ready for sleep. At the end of this poem or song, there appears a final eight-line stanza, demarcated by italics, that goes back through each character in the preceding stanzas to repeat the advice, "now close your eyes." While the entire text is unclear in genre, so too is the final stanza possibly a poem, possibly a song. Here, Brown continues to layer her writing, providing a richer, fuller artistic experience. Similarly, "All the Pretty Little Horses" follows "Close Your Eyes," and although this text is not defined either, *The Golden Sleepy Book* includes an Acknowledgment above its copyright that reads,

> The author learned the song 'All the Pretty Little Horses' from Mammy Ludy Ludy Hinton and Sugar Meat Hinton of Halifax, Virginia. A somewhat different version has been copyrighted by the late John Lomax. The version that appears in this book is printed with his kind permission.

Child readers in 1948 may have been familiar with this popular American lullaby, ascribed to African American origins before the Civil War. If not, then the Acknowledgment would be the only indication that this text is a song until readers turn the page and a number of shifts occur. Visually, the second page of the song appears in black and white instead of color. In addition, the final lyrics are encased by the wooden railings of a corral. Printed on the railings, almost as a sign, are the words "Baby's Song." And under those words appear two lines of sheet music with the lyrics printed within. The page's structure indicates that Baby's Song is a separate text from the "Pretty Little Horses" song above it, but the lyrics remain the same, so it is unclear what the title Baby's Song means. Nonetheless, this moment offers musical notation within a song within a picture book that also includes narrative and poetry. Brown's Modern melding of genres and forms accesses distinct artistic mediums to yield a beautiful collage of expression. Finally, the last two pieces in *The Golden Sleepy Book* include a final narrative of the different ways animals and insects go to sleep as well as a concluding poem or song called "Whip-Poor-Will." Italicized and written as a single, centered stanza, this closing text leaves its genre undefined, emphasizing the indeterminate nature of this artwork but also the ingenuous partnership of the multi-genre text and a child's experience of the world.

Clearly, Margaret Wise Brown worked as more than an author of children's books. Her interests ranged into visual art, philosophy, and music, and at her death in 1952, she was producing collaborative art that valued a wide range of disciplines. Her exploration of sound and music for children was still escalating, and some of the musical projects we now enjoy stand as interpretations of her work rather than direct products of her intentions. As one of her fields of inquiry, however, musical art reflects Brown herself in some ways as the "non-referential way music creates meanings that have the potential to be timeless, universal and able to communicate human, emotional truths" also refers to Brown's picture books (Moss xiv). Without demanding that her words always directly, explicitly convey literal meaning for a child audience and without even defining the genres in which she worked, Margaret Wise Brown manifested her regard for a child's ability to participate in art and her belief that her audience deserved quality representation.

Notes

1 In *The Cambridge Companion to Modernism*, for example, Daniel Albright joins other Modernist scholars in his designation of music as "the vanguard act" in Modernism (241).

2 The term "intermediality" appears in a number of scholarship areas, the two most common remaining art studies and digital media studies. While some disciplines use the term to refer to convergence among media in film or technology, this chapter uses the designation to indicate places where different forms of art overlap in ways that contribute to a shared space.

3 This term "melopoeia" finds its coining in a 1968 Ezra Pound essay where he designates three aspects of poetry; melopoeia is poetry that includes words that carry musical properties (25). I use it here to refer to the crossroads between writing and music.

4 A third reason for interest among writers in music was the possibility for social change. Scholar Gemma Moss explains that "many modernists—writers who were deeply invested in producing social change through literature because of the many problems they saw in contemporary life—turn to an abstract art form like music" (x). This turn in music originated in Richard Wagner's belief in art as social agent, but that reason is less important in children's picture books and does not mirror Brown's themes in significant ways.

5 In writing on Gertrude Stein, Marianne DeKoven determines Stein's experimentation with words as melody "fruitless," even as it continues to represent an important historical "investigati[on of] the possibilities of writing as a form of music" (165). The presence of these experiments found both positive and negative receptions.

6 Tim Armstrong also emphasizes the "modernist preoccupation with embodied aesthetics [...] modernism's depiction of somatic experience and streams of consciousness" (119). This focus on embodiment might also lend itself to a smooth fit in children's literature whose readers often find themselves learning about their bodies in the world.

References

Adorno, Theodor. "Music, Language, and Composition." *The Musical Quarterly*, 77, 3, 1993, pp. 401–14.

Albright, Daniel. "Musical motives in Modernism." *The Cambridge Companion to Modernism*, edited by Michael Levenson, 2nd ed. Cambridge UP, 2011.

Armstrong, Tim. "Modernism and Music." *The Bloomsbury Companion to Modernist Literature*, edited by Ulrika Maude & Mark Nixon. Bloomsbury, 2018, pp. 119–35.

Badar, Barbara. *American Picture Books from Noah's Ark to the Beast Within.* Macmillan, 1976.

Bonner, David. *Revolutionizing Children's Records: The Young People's Records and Children's Record Guild Series, 1946–1977*. Scarecrow, 2007.

Brown, Margaret Wise. *Goodnight Songs*, edited by Amy Gary. Sterling, 2014.

———. *Goodnight Songs: A Celebration of the Seasons*, edited by Amy Gary, Sterling, 2015.

———. *Long Time That I've Loved You*. Silver Dolphin, 2020.

———. *Love Song of the Little Bear*. Hyperion, 2001.

———. "Stories to be Sung and Songs to be Told." *The Book of Knowledge Annual: 1952*. Grolier Society, 1952, pp. 166–70.

———. *The Golden Sleepy Book*. Simon & Schuster, 1948.

———. *The Little Brass Band*, illustrated by Clement Hurd. Harper, 1948.

———. *The Noisy Book*. Harper, 1939.

———. *The Quiet Noisy Book*. Harper, 1950.

———. *The Runaway Bunny*, illustrated by Clement Hurd. Harper, 1942.

———. *Wait Till the Moon Is Full*, illustrated by Garth Williams. Harper, 1948.

DeKoven, Marianne. "Melody." *Modern Critical Views: Gertrude Stein*, edited by Harold Bloom. Chelsea House, 1986. pp. 165–75.

Derveaux, Marc. "The Sonority of Language in Literary and Musical Modernity." *Music and Literary Modernism*, edited by Robert McParland. Cambridge Scholars, 2006, pp. 4–11.

Jung, Julie. *Revisionary Rhetoric, Feminist Pedagogy, and Multigenre Texts*. Southern Illinois UP, 2005.

Marcus, Leonard S. *Margaret Wise Brown: Awakened by the Moon*. Beacon, 1992.

Maude, Ulrika. "Introduction: Modernism, Experimentation and Form." *The Bloomsbury Companion to Modernist Literature*, edited by Ulrika Maude & Mark Nixon. Bloomsbury, 2018, pp. 1–18.

McParland, Robert. "Introduction." *Music and Literary Modernism: Critical Essays and Comparative Studies*, edited by Robert McParland, 2nd ed. Cambridge Scholars, 2009, pp. 1–2.

Moss, Gemma. *Modernism, Music and the Politics of Aesthetics*. Edinburgh UP, 2021.

Oxford English Dictionary. "Prosody. 1a." *The Oxford English Dictionary*. Oxford UP, 2023.

Pound, Ezra. *Literary Essays of Ezra Pound*. New Directions, 1968.

Susina, Jan. "Children's Reading, Repetition, and Rereading: Gertrude Stein, Margaret Wise Brown, and Goodnight Moon." *Second Thoughts: A Focus on Rereading*, edited by David Galef. Wayne State UP, 1998, pp. 115–25.

Epilogue

I knew very little about Margaret Wise Brown until I had my second child. With each of my two children, I found myself spending quite a bit of time with board books and picture books, not only to educate and entertain them, but also to put them to sleep. When my daughter was born, I pulled back out the books I had collected five years before, at my son's birth, but gradually discovered that I would go back again and again to certain texts I enjoyed and which seemed to calm my children at night. When I compared the authors, I found that I had repeatedly chosen Margaret Wise Brown books. I was familiar already with *Goodnight Moon* and *The Runaway Bunny* from my own childhood, but these were not the stories I most respected. Instead, it was *The Color Kittens*, *The Friendly Book*, *The Train to Timbuctoo*, *The Wonderful House* regularly sitting next to the rocking chair in our nursery. As an English professor with a PhD in children's literature, my interest naturally led me to begin researching this author, and the new stories I found in her collection only increased my absorption. Texts such as *The Important Book*, *The Golden Sleepy Book*, and *Our World* began to captivate me as I read and re-read them, finding that they give and give with each read; they address multiple audiences, convey complicated themes, unite highly developed art forms, and ask poignant questions that seemed both too advanced for children's picture books and exactly right for the genre. I realized that this project might take me a few years.

My daughter is now nine years old, and I have not lost any enthusiasm in studying Margaret Wise Brown. Brown was a fascinating person, and two brilliant biographies have been published about her by Leonard Marcus, a preeminent historian, and Amy Gary, an accessible

DOI: 10.4324/9781032727028-6

publisher. While Brown's story certainly informs her work, and I would jump at the chance to have a meal and chat with her, it remains the books themselves that draw me in. The quality of her texts has not suffered over time. They remain relevant, and they remain readable. I must admit that I probably am working through her collection with distinct focus, as I have found myself disappointed time and time again recently with scholarship in my field. When I first entered the children's literature discipline in 2008 as a new PhD student with a background in Southern literature, I found a fresh, inquisitive, welcoming academic field that practiced strenuous scholarship on worthy yet oft-overlooked texts. Since then, children's literature scholarship has grown more and more focused on the usefulness of the text, on the social change scholars hope the book will encourage, rather than on a more balanced assessment of its use, its craft, its context, and its effect. This newer, more narrow, activist focus seems to have lowered the standard of textual accomplishment. Instead of considering what is said in light of how it is said, the weight of scrutiny has shifted almost exclusively to content at the expense of the story's achievement in other areas. In addition to Brown's short but lively past, her books encourage repeated readings. As textual products, they request and deserve examination beyond their social use.

And therein lies the question of the books written by Brown that have been published posthumously. Barbara Badar points out that Brown's collaborations were still held to the author's high standards: "Of special interest for the history of Young Scott [the publisher], though, are the books published after Brown's death in 1952, without the participation of the exacting author" ("William" 461). Can a genuine Margaret Wise Brown book be published after her death? Her ideas, her preferences, were so strong that it may not be possible for an interpretation of her style, her work, or her wishes to match the real thing. Yet that task is what several publishing companies have taken on, as more and more Brown manuscripts continue to appear with new, publisher-chosen illustrations. For the HarperCollins program called Explore the World of Margaret Wise Brown, begun in 2016, some texts were scheduled and assigned "some of the most recognized illustrators of our times," but in other cases, HarperCollins chose illustrators before deciding what book to allocate them (Lodge pars. 1, 9). In those cases, it would appear that Brown's texts do not take priority; instead, the illustrators' prominence, combined with Brown's name as a marketing tool, achieves the publication goal.

This is not to argue that books published after Brown's death are all necessarily bad, but it is to argue that they are not necessarily good and should probably face a closer look before being accepted as a Margaret Wise Brown creation. Brown respected children. She never had any of her own, and she may never have even known them in great enough intimacy to hallow them. Instead, she studied them, had friendships with some, but more than anything, she felt as if she were one of them. That difference may largely explain the shift her books have taken since her death, as most now include a preciosity absent in her work, for, "although adults often sentimentalize small animals and children, the animals and children are not sentimental about themselves, and Brown was not sentimental about them either" (Rahn 151). Increasing Western insulation of the child finds its way into newly published Brown books, changing the art's aesthetics and tone from what the author pursued during her career.

When providing Brown's texts the time they earn, the quality of art that Brown requested for her young audience grows apparent. And recognition of that quality and the standard Brown established demonstrates possibilities among young audiences of responding to complicated ideas through artworks. These possibilities certainly reflect a veracity in ideas about art as communication beyond linguistics. Where some purposes may not translate easily to children in words, art can bridge gaps in understanding. In fact, Stanton argues that Brown's "invention of the 'noisy book' genre and her desire for strong visual and tactile qualities in books were related to her belief that children are, in some important respects, more aesthetically sophisticated than adults" ("Goodnight" 8). From these perspectives, the picture book is an ideal space for cultured art. Not only that, but a child audience may also remain an ideal audience for Modernist works. While Modernism is often described by such terms as "repetition, rhythm, absurdism, changes in perspective, a subjective point of view, a rejection of sentimentality," and "blurring of genre, flagrancy of theme, disobedience to old artistic rules," even "an aesthetics of transitoriness and immanence, whose central values are change and novelty," definitions or descriptions of childhood experience could fit the same, exact phrasing (Holmes par. 24; Albright 37; Călinescu 3). While Brown herself thought, worked, and wrote in a Modern context, the triumph of her art appears to express the greater truth that subjective childhood experience is also a Modern experience. This is not to denigrate Modernism but to elevate the child. The confusion, the gaps and fragments, the recognition of beauty and deconstruction of language, the desire for novelty and observation of life's fragility all connect childhood with Modernist aims. Scholars recognize that "modernism has often been considered a stylistic rather than a temporal movement, and one of its most striking features is its salient formal experimentation" (Maude 1). This style may also best represent the impressions of the young as they fight to understand the world they've been born into. With much of children's picture books offering collaborations of artists aiming to capture the commonly disjointed impressions of the child reader and then extending possible meanings and purposes to these impressions, the picture book may represent an essential Modern genre. Rather than relegate Modernism to the early twentieth century, scholars may benefit from seeing this historically bounded movement as extended into a stylistic continuum:

> To reduce modernism to a generation collapses it to a biological bulge like the baby boom or consigns it to the symptoms of mass behavior like the Roaring Twenties. Pinning a date on modernism risks reducing art to the artless by-product of fashion and historical determination, a condition that undoubtedly applies to most art in any period.
>
> (Rasula 3)

One of Margaret Wise Brown's most lasting legacies may be her unwitting elevation of the picture book to Modern art form and her experimentations with its expressive possibilities.

In 1946, Margaret Wise Brown was named in *Life* magazine as the "World's Most Prolific Picture-Book Writer" (Holmes par. 1). She worked also in fields of visual art, music, and educational philosophy, and many of her texts inspired generations of picture book art. Yet, she is often left off lists of "Best Picture Book Authors" and even "Most Prolific Picture Book Authors of All Time."[1] A possible reason for these oversights is her relegation to the past, maybe even her success in imbuing much of the culture and milieu of her time. Yet, her texts remain effective, expressive, poignant, and relevant, largely due to the style she practiced. The problem may not be Brown's embodiment of Modernism but our contemporary oversight of Modernism's endowment, for, while culture and experience have changed, much about childhood subjectivity has not changed, and because of her work, Margaret Wise Brown continues to deserve the designation of "children's literature royalty" (Christian Robinson qtd. in Lodge par. 6).

Note

1 These lists are easily found with simple Google searches on such sites as Reading Rockets, Epic, and Book Riot. Although possibly unreliable sources, which explains their inaccuracies, these are often the sources used for public searches, influencing market choices and narrowing audience access.

References

Albright, Daniel. "Musical motives in Modernism." *The Cambridge Companion to Modernism*, edited by Michael Levenson, 2nd ed. Cambridge UP, 2011.

Badar, Barbara. "William R. Scott, publisher." *Horn Book Magazine*, 74, 4, Jul/Aug 1998, pp. 459–64.

Călinescu, Matei. *Five Faces of Modernity: Modernism, Avant-Garde, Decadence, Kitsch, Postmodernism*. Duke UP, 1987.

Holmes, Anna. "The Radical Woman Behind 'Goodnight Moon.'" Onward and Upward with the Arts, *The New Yorker*, 31 January 2022, accessed October 2023, pars. 54.

Lodge, Sally. "HarperCollins Rolls Out New Margaret Wise Brown Line." *Publishers Weekly*, 11 February 2016, accessed October 2023, pars. 13.

Maude, Ulrika. "Introduction: Modernism, Experimentation and Form." *The Bloomsbury Companion to Modernist Literature*, edited by Ulrika Maude & Mark Nixon. Bloomsbury, 2018, pp. 1–18.

Rahn, Suzanne. "Cat-Quest: A Symbolic Animal in Margaret Wise Brown." *Children's Literature*, 22, 1994, pp. 149–61.

Rasula, Jed. *History of a Shiver: The Sublime Impudence of Modernism*. Oxford UP, 2016.

Stanton, Joseph. "Goodnight Nobody: Comfort and the Vast Dark in the Poems of Margaret Wise Brown and her Collaborators." *The Important Book: Children's Picture Books as Art and Literature*. Scarecrow, 2005, pp. 7–17.

Index

Note: Page numbers in *italic* refers to Figures.

For Product Safety Concerns and Information please contact our EU representative GPSR@taylorandfrancis.com
Taylor & Francis Verlag GmbH, Kaufingerstraße 24, 80331 München, Germany

www.ingramcontent.com/pod-product-compliance
Lightning Source LLC
LaVergne TN
LVHW010917110826
845149LV00013B/2401

* 9 7 8 1 0 3 2 7 2 7 0 4 2 *